Aber Pron

I dedicate this book to the memory of my parents,
Maurice and Gwen Henley, who loved the promenade.

Gyrru lawr y ffyrdd bach cul
I'r prom, atgofion melys sydd
Wrth edrych allan o'r cyfarwydd dir
Ar fachlud mwyn ar ddiwedd dydd.

Dewis mainc a chodi llaw
Ar gyfeillion agos fan hyn, fan draw.
Diolchaf i'r ddau mewn munud ddistaw
Am yr atgofion hapus i'm calon i a ddaw.

Catherine Alys Henley

Aber Prom

A pictorial history of events and entertainment on Aberystwyth promenade

Peter Henley

y Lolfa

I give my special thanks and acknowledgement to the many people, locally and nationwide, who have offered me encouragement and willing help during my researches for the book. In particular, I would like to thank Michael Freeman, Curator of the Ceredigion Museum, for his continual support and encouragement; the staff of the National Library of Wales; the Archives Office at the County Offices in Aberystwyth and the staff at the Town's reference library.

Peter Henley

First impression: 2007

© Peter Henley and Y Lolfa Cyf., 2007

This book is subject to copyright and may not be reproduced by any means except for review purposes without the prior written consent of the publishers.

Design: Alan Thomas
Cover: Robat Gruffudd

ISBN: 978 086243 984 2
ISBN-10: 0 86243 984 1
Printed on acid-free and partly recycled paper
and published and bound in Wales by
Y Lolfa Cyf., Talybont, Ceredigion SY24 5AP
e-mail ylolfa@ylolfa.com
website www.ylolfa.com
tel 01970 832 304
fax 832 782

Preface

Aberystwyth promenade has played a very important part in the life of Aberystwyth's inhabitants and visitors since it was first built in about 1819. It provides a place to take exercise and show off; it forms a boundary between land and sea, safety and peril, decorum and abandon. For some it is a place of work and for others a place of unrestrained freedom and enjoyment.

Although on the very edge of the town, it was, for many, the main attraction. Despite official control, a great variety of entertainment was provided along it. From as early as the 1830s it attracted entertainers who came for the brief season to perform to the small number of affluent visitors. Once the railways arrived in the 1860s, vast numbers of people arrived on special day excursions or for a week and many of them must have spent much of their time on the prom. The University gradually took over a number of buildings on the sea front, assuring not only the success of the town out of season, but an extended, lively use of the prom during term time.

The complex history of the entertainment provided along the prom for nearly 200 years has been thoroughly researched by Peter Henley. He has placed it in the context of entertainment elsewhere in Britain and also describes many of the other activities that were on offer to the promenaders.

This book is an important contribution to the history of the town.

Michael Freeman
Curator, Ceredigion Museum.

AUTHOR DETAILS

I was born in Gwalia House, 62 North Parade, Aberystwyth, in 1938, next door to a very busy Gwalia Garage and petrol station belonging to my Grandfather, the poet Charles Abel Jones, and his four sons. On leaving Ardwyn Grammar School in 1956, I became an apprentice mechanic there, involving myself in most aspects of garage life. In 1959, I became a member of the University Botany Department's technical staff and followed a career there, initially, as a Scientific Photographer and Electron Microscopist, and, later, as a Chief Technician in the Institute of Biological Sciences. During my lifetime in Aberystwyth, I became a member of the RNLI lifeboat crew, and Chairman of the Camera Club and the Ceredigion Art Society. I am also an amateur musician, photographer and artist, and a committee member of the local Civic Society. I live in Bow Street with my wife Dinah. We have two daughters, who graduated in the Universities of Aberystwyth and Swansea. My passion to record the history of the promenade began when I was invited, along with David Jenkins and David Williams, to provide the first exhibition for the newly opened Welsh Industrial and Maritime Museum in Cardiff. My contribution included the restored work of the photographer Emile Thomas Evans, depicting Edwardian Aberystwyth.

CONTENTS

11	The Growth Of Aberystwyth As A Resort
16	Music History
	Bands
	Minstrels
	Beach Performers
	Castle Entertainment
	Concert Parties
	Dance Bands
	Pop Groups
120	Punch & Judy
124	Bathing
130	Donkeys
134	Pleasure Boats
149	Photographers
154	Food
161	Carnival
165	Early Transport
170	Crowds
172	Constitution Hill

174	Religious Events
178	The University and the Prom
183	Royal Visits
186	Military Bands
190	Naval Visits
196	Air Displays
202	Aberystwyth Lifeboat
210	Beach Lifesaving
212	Kicking The Bar
215	Seagulls
216	References

INTRODUCTION

The character of every British seaside resort, the resultant cast from the mould of time and influence, is an indication of past initiatives, taken not only by its residents and controlling authorities wishing to develop their locality as an attraction, but also by those from afar attracted to them.

The resulting impression left upon the seaside towns by the annual influx of summer visitors shaped and labelled their existence. To emphasise the point, a comparison between the few Welsh resorts, after two hundred years as pleasure seeking venues, can be made by considering their relative proximities to areas of population. Aberystwyth, as a result of its greater distance from major towns and cities, developed a unique character of its own. The demand upon the town was less than that placed upon the north Wales resorts of Llandudno and Rhyl, which were relatively closer to large cities. It didn't share in the consequent requirement to expand as a large scale entertainment centre capable of accommodating and entertaining greater numbers of people.

Within that uniqueness, Aberystwyth has since offered a level of seaside enjoyment within a scale appropriate to its size as a resort. In the equally short lifetime of development, it took the initiative to construct an arena for the summer pleasure-seeker, namely, the 'Promenade'.

Many of the principal coastal resorts in the United Kingdom share a common description for that exclusively delightful area where the land meets the sea: 'The Promenade'. The use of the word could easily be considered as a convenient way of describing a pedestrian way or esplanade that was simply functional and not necessarily at the seaside. *In situ,* it could also be considered a sea defence walkway, or a neat perimeter wall isolating a beach from the inhabited area of a town. The Oxford dictionary describes the word as: *'A walk, or sometimes a ride or drive, taken especially for display, leisure, etcetera.'*

By those who share its existence, it is affectionately referred to as *'The Prom'*, the one-and-a-half-mile length of road and pavement that has survived in its entirety, principally unchanged, for over one hundred years. Initially, Aberystwyth was one of only three significant coastal resorts in Wales and, by 1800, by virtue of its isolation, was somewhat exclusive. The other two, Swansea and Tenby, developed as bathing places from the late 18th century, but Swansea's future direction soon succumbed to the pollution produced by the copper refineries and potteries. The earliest principal users of Welsh seaside resorts were from the wealthy and leisured classes. The town wasn't well equipped initially to receive these distinguished visitors but, regardless of the limited amenities, the visitors said that the Welsh hospitality was one of the town's chief attractions. Not everyone appreciated the long journey by horse-drawn coach from across the border. One Oxford student clearly displayed his feelings, in the Devil's Bridge Hotel register at that period:

> 'After jumbling and jotting o'er Cambria's rough roads
> This spot makes us ample amends;
> If the devil thus ornaments all his abodes,
> No wonder he has so many friends.'

In 1839, the writer Alfred Lord Tennyson, at the age of thirty, stayed in Aberystwyth at 'The Inn on the Terrace', no doubt, the Royal Belle Vue Hotel, during the pangs of separation from his fiancée, Emily. Of the town he wrote: *'This place, The Cambrian Brighton, pleases me not. A sea, certainly today, of a most lovely blue but with scarce a ripple. Anything more unlike the old Homeric 'much sounding' sea I never saw. Yet the bay is said to be tempestuous.'*

The visitor's prime interest would have been the pursuit of health-promoting activities such as sea bathing and walking, rather than typically organised promenade attractions. To entice the more modest into the sea, bathing machines appeared on the beaches in about 1810. The appreciation awarded to visitors who had travelled great distances to stay in the town during the summer months, in mid-Victorian times, is understandable. It is extraordinary to find that winter months apparently did not deter the obviously hardy travellers from coming. A report in the local press of Saturday January 28th, 1860 stated: *'The town early on Monday morning presented a very lively appearance, from the constant arrival of visitors from the surrounding districts, which filled the hotels to overflowing. Still, however, by dint of good management on the part of the hotel keepers, accommodation was provided for every one.'*

The town became the nearest resort for most of central Wales and the Midlands, following the arrival of the Railway in 1864. The numbers of visitors drawn to the seaside, therefore, increased enormously and, as a result, it became less exclusive. The resort attracted, like other resorts, a greater number of families from humbler backgrounds, although Aberystwyth did not appear to take on a plebeian character, unlike those resorts closer geographically to large British cities. A conflict between the needs of the original, discerning type of visitor and the new tripper developed, while entrepreneurs, regardless of the fact, added many of the facilities that were to be found in other resorts, principally, the promenade itself. To satisfy all who clamoured for the seaside, the developing catalyst and much heralded attraction was, of course, the associated entertainment.

THE GROWTH OF ABERYSTWYTH AS A RESORT

For five hundred years, the people of Aberystwyth lived within the confines of the town walls that had been erected when the castle was built, between 1277 and 1289. Building elsewhere, outside the walls, on the common land known as *Morfa Swnd*, or Sand Marsh, was initially inhibited until 1797, when the Corporation succumbed to the ever increasing need for accommodation by visitors. The town developed with the building of many new houses, not only along the shore line towards Constitution Hill, but also around the perimeter of the town wall.

In England, George III began a new trend in 1787, when, following advice from his doctors, he went from London to Weymouth, to bathe in the sea. The event was greeted by the public with great celebration as the monarch took to the water, hoping to improve his health. It was accepted by the aping, general public as a completely new departure, and a visit to the seaside became a nationwide annual event.

The importance placed by the physicians of the 18th and 19th century upon staying at health-maintaining spa towns, whether inland or on the coast, prompted Dr Henry Bell, the Aberystwyth Infirmary physician, in 1861, to advertise the benefits in a book entitled: *'An Edition of Hints and Suggestions respecting sea-side Influence on impaired health and disease.'* It was a successful publication, apparently running into several editions.

The early visitors to Aberystwyth were primarily interested in pursuits that would be regarded as healthy. They were principally walkers, artists and writers, seeking out the picturesque, with time and the ability to pay the high costs of travel to Wales.

The Corporation of the Town owned most of the land along the seashore at Aberystwyth and were reluctant to allow any unregulated building. Wealthy gentry, wishing to spend their summertime near the coast, would enjoy socialising away from home and would seek to meet with members of their same class in the town. It was generally felt that the building of summer houses locally would meet these interests. One particular person was Sir Uvedale Price, of Croft Castle in Herefordshire. In 1788, he sought permission from the Corporation to build on the cliff near the castle. It was the first house to be built along this coast and also the first to be built outside the walls of the mediaeval town. It stood within the locality of today's Cambria Conference Centre and heralded the beginnings of the town as a resort. To complement the fine views that could be enjoyed from the front windows of this house, the very first part of the sea wall was built in front of it. This venture would culminate in its continuation as a sea wall and promenade that ultimately ran for more than one and a half miles, from the harbour to Constitution Hill. It was completed in about

Aber Prom

1795. The continuation of house-building and a public promenade, where Marine Terrace is today, began about 1819 and rapidly continued northward. By 1848, there were nearly sixty houses along the terrace.

In 1797, the magistrate and traveller Henry Wigstead visited Aberystwyth with the London satirist and artist Thomas Rowlandson, in preparation for an illustrated account of a short tour of Wales. Wigstead's description of the town, *The Brighton of Wales*, implies that it provided many of the facilities that late 18th century visitors required. It vied well with established spa towns and watering places such as Brighton, Weymouth and Bath, with the advantage that its isolation from much of the rest of Britain (despite the construction of new turnpike roads from the 1770s) made it somewhat exclusive.

Towards the end of the 18th century, there was little for the visitor to do. Throughout their summer sojourn, they would have sampled all the walks, the entertainment and the church services. One discerning visitor anonymously wrote of his stay in 1802: *'I must confess, the sea did not come up to the idea I had formed of it when we first saw it. It was low water and calm. I saw it again in the evening when it was high water but even then it did not astonish me so much as I expected; but I think it a very grand sight.'*

On Sunday, he and his companions went to church, bathed and walked, and stated: *'The day passed off as well as we could have expected in so dull a place.'*

The following day: *'We left Aberystwyth tolerably satisfied with our stay at that place.'* (Anon. A journal of a tour thro' North Wales, begun 7th June 1802, NLW MS 789B p.19)

A Mrs Hutton and her daughter, Catherine, stayed in the Talbot Hotel in Market Street in 1787, but were encouraged by the landlord to go elsewhere, when it was found that they were not spending enough. *'We ate our boiled chicken, or a mutton chop, till it was found that we did not drink a sufficient quantity of wine with it, and a hint was given us of a private lodging. We took the hint and soon after the lodging where we had a small parlour, a large chamber with two beds, a very good dinner, and bread and butter for 16 shillings a week.'* Catherine Hutton ended the account of her visit by stating: *'Aberystwyth was the only place I ever left wishing that I might not see it again.'* (Birmingham City Archives: Hutton and Beale families of Birmingham MS 3597)

Thomas Turner was much more complimentary, following his stay in 1837: *'Another week has too quickly passed away in the enjoyment of this very delightful coast, and we shall now soon bid adieu to scenes which have been more than usually captivating. Having been highly favoured by a fine season, by the society of several friends, visitors like ourselves to the place, by every accommodation afforded at our lodgings and by the beauty and variety of our own excursions abroad, we must experience much regret at our departure.'* (Thomas Turner, Narrative of a journey associated with a Fly, from Gloucester to Aberystwyth and from Aberystwyth through North Wales, 1837. p.39).

By 1820, Aberystwyth had all the facilities that a visitor would expect to find in a spa town: a fine music room, a theatre and extensive public walks. In comparison with other major coastal resorts, the development was slow, principally as a result of the poor roads that led to the town. Ceredigion was almost the last county in Wales to have a Turnpike act, in 1770, and the last to be joined to the railway system, in 1864. By the 1880s, the resort was on the brink of the Victorian clamour for the seaside. The ability to reach the seaside had now become possible for everyone. The era of the day trip had arrived. The ease with which a family could reach the coast by train was quickly adopted. Thousands would pour into the resort, all eager to reach the sea and, of course, to be entertained. The general public were now rather more interested in the available entertainment than their health, which the earlier, more fashionable society had been. Their enjoyment would have been to stroll along the promenade to the sound of music, whether it was the ever popular brass band or otherwise.

The bank holiday act of 1871 allowed a greater freedom for the general public, entitling them to five public holidays a year. Amazingly, it was to be another 68 years, in 1938, before paid holidays in Britain were introduced. For many, the holiday was still unattainable, due to low wages and high unemployment. The day trip would survive for some time, for those able to get to the seaside easily.

By the end of the 19th century, Aberystwyth compared favourably with the bigger resorts, with an elegant promenade, a pier with a large elaborate pavilion, bandstands, a park on the castle grounds and Constitution Hill. Within the town there was a skating rink, a theatre and several places of entertainment. By that period, there were several large hotels and numerous lodging houses along the terrace.

The summer clamour for the seaside and the required accommodation, during this annual influx of visitors to the town, was high on the agenda of the Aberystwyth Borough Council, early each year. Consideration was also given towards providing ample beach space for the expected crowds that would pour out of the trains and charabancs and head for the shore, in particular Marine Terrace, from the Pier Pavilion to Constitution Hill. The contractual and limited musical entertainment provided would be the result of tenders invited via the press. From the enterprising entertainer, it meant a courteous letter to the Mayor and Town Clerk, explaining the type of sea-side attraction they wished to provide on the promenade or the beach. The approach by later, casual performers would often be turned down. In September 1913, the secretary of the Rheidol United Choir benevolently offered to the council the services of the choir, to sing on the beach one evening and collect for a local boatman Mr Henry Jones, who was in ill-health. It was resolved in council committee: *'That having regard to the limited extent of the beach, the application be turned down.'*

The attractiveness and attractions of the promenade were of paramount importance to the local council, whose responsibility it was to maintain its continuing appeal with unimpeded views for the

Detail of an 1832 engraving from a painting by Walker of the developing promenade at Aberystwyth. The shape of the walkway and line of houses are easily recognisable along Victoria and Marine Terrace, although the promenade has yet to be built to its full width and length. Collection: National Library of Wales

regular and prospective visitors. On the 26th of June 1894 it was reported in the local newspaper that:
'The council has resolved that it is absolutely essential that in the interests of the town that no obstruction should be allowed on the Marine Terrace or beach which in any way is calculated to impair the uninterrupted view to the sea.'

Emphasising the need to maintain the sea view from the houses on the terrace, it was reported in the same issue: *'It was resolved that the Proprietor of the recently erected covered bandstand be requested on or before Tuesday next to remove so much of the same as is higher than the promenade.'*

The visitors and locals were offered a galaxy of entertainment throughout the year, provided by minstrels, pierrots, theatrical acts and plays, and Welsh musical concerts. During the first half of the twentieth century, these attractions were augmented by fairground and amusement arcades and by a new Art Deco Bandstand and Municipal Hall.

Local people and children on the promenade in about 1860. The photographer would have stood at the lower end of Pier Street, with Rock House in the foreground. Although the houses appear unchanged, the promenade perimeter and surface will have changed considerably by the 20th century. Collection: Nigel Davies. Photographer unknown

MUSIC HISTORY

EARLY LOCAL MUSIC

The introduction of music within the modern locality of Aberystwyth can be considered as being from the 13th century, coinciding with the completion of the Edwardian Castle, built on a site chosen in 1277, in the newly formed town of Llanbadarn Gaerog, so-called to distinguish it from the neighbouring town of Llanbadarn Fawr. Up until the fourteenth century, the development of music could have taken two separate paths; initially, at the previously established Episcopal parish church at Llanbadarn Fawr, within the ancient commotes of Penweddig and Vaenor, and, secondly, within the walls of the new castle. From 1188, the Church had need of sacred music, and possibly relied upon local musicians. Otherwise, the requirements of Chapel service and Court entertainment in the nearby developing castle would have been met by imported musicians, probably gleemen, whose presence in the country dates from the 8th century. They would have played simple stringed instruments, sometimes accompanied by a harp, horn or pipe, with jugglers and dancers often performing to the music. The Castle court's needs would have changed little in comparison with the several changes of occupancy, by the Normans, then, the men of Ceredigion and Owain Glyndwr. Norman occupation of the Castle continued after the rebellion, until the 17th century and the Civil War, and its destruction by the Parliamentarians in 1649. The town within the castle walls survived; its occupants, now integrated into the locality and free of hostility, became a community prepared for adaptation to a new interloper era, that of the holiday-maker and tourist.

The musical influence from the nearby settlement of Trefechan on the increasing number of indigenous Welsh inhabitants within the walls would not have been affected significantly until the fourteenth century. During the Middle Ages, groups of musicians were forming and were generally known as minstrels. They were professional entertainers, having the ability to supplement their musical ability with acrobatics, juggling or story-telling.

The heyday of minstrelsy lasted from c. 1250 to 1500. The Welsh minstrels in the 16th century were described as *Y Beirdd,* the Bards, with the ability to play either the *Crwth,* a simple stringed instrument, described as early as 600 AD in a poem by Fortunas, or the harp, by the ever popular ballad singer.

The independent and established tradition of Welsh minstrelsy, distinguished by Hywel Dda (Hywel the Good) c. 950 AD as *Y Pencerdd*, the Chief of Song in the local bardic fraternity, or *Bardd teulu*, the family bard, formed an equally important part of the court of kings, princes and chieftains in other districts of Wales.

Minstrels generally had no fixed abode and owed no allegiance to civil or ecclesiastical authority; the

Music History

Owain Glyndŵr with his family at his court at Sycharth, depicted in a watercolour painting by Margaret Jones. Collection: NLW

earliest of them were known as *Jongleurs*, a mixture of singer and clown. It is known that King Edward I, who instigated the building of Aberystwyth Castle, ordered 426 jongleurs to perform at his daughter's wedding. The Bard, a very popular figure, responsible for the development of secular music in Wales, was a repository of family histories, stories, legends, songs and poetry of the people. His arrival at a venue would be regarded with pleasure and he would be given a warm welcome. He was an educated person, totally conversant with tradition, and relied upon to provide the latest news for the court.

The success and fortunes of the minstrels through the following centuries went through many changes. Later types of entertainer, known as *Troubadours*, came from Provence, in France, and were lyric-poets, or poet musicians. Far from being a carefree vagabond, the troubadour was a characteristically serious, well educated entertainer, whose art was one in which music and poetry became associated with the courtly ideal. The troubadours were often attached to one castle, and were generally noted from the 12th to the 13th centuries. They would play pipes and a tabor, a type of two-skinned drum, slung around the waist and played with wooden sticks. They would be expected to sing, read and provide news for the entertainment of their master and mistress.

By the 14th century, a relaxation in the law gave minstrels and troubadours the opportunity to play locally at fairs and galas.

Many of these early entertainers gave up their formal employment and made their solitary way across the country, working as itinerant musicians, seeking work at fairs, tournaments and weddings. They played an important role in traditional culture, supplying news as well as music. Their role included the spread of knowledge of songs and brought musical expertise within the locality.

In the 16th century, an act of Queen Elizabeth I classed all wandering minstrels as '*rogues, vagabonds and sturdy beggars*' and required them, as itinerant musicians, to wear cloaks and the badges of their patrons, to denote whom they served. The distinctive attire would help to prevent them wandering off to play at 'unfavourable venues'. The Ruritarian, gold-braided uniform of the world-wide, modern, military bandsman is a legacy of those times and owes its modern existence to those early employers.

The emerging bands of entertainers owed their existence to the tradition of itinerant musicianship, which survived the rulings of local councils that banished and persecuted vagrants, forcing them in severe cases, from the country. This treatment encouraged many of the nomadic minstrels to settle in one location. They later banded together into guilds, to protect their interests. The Elizabethan poor laws severely restricted their movements, failing to distinguish them from landless beggars. Although later laws were less oppressive, the itinerants were never to regain their prestige of former days. Paradoxically, the tradition of itinerant musicianship survived unchallenged at that time in Wales.

In castellated towns similar to Aberystwyth, before the 14th century, the town gate keepers and night watchmen would have been given a musical instrument, such as a horn, to sound an alarm, to signal that all was well, or announce the hour or the weather. This is certainly a practice that is unnecessary today, but, regardless of the disturbance then, the knowledge that all was well in the night was of great importance to the sleeping community.

Music History

A character sketch of itinerant musicians, from a volume by George Orleans Delamotte. Swansea 1818. Collection: National Library of Wales

Collectively, they became known as *'The Waits'*, and, by the end of the 14th century, they were hired to play for civic functions and religious services. Their instruments varied, although the *Shawm* or *wait-pipe*, a rather loud and penetrating wind instrument, was very common. The *Sackbut, Curtal* and *Cornett* came later, all capable of being played cacophonously to great effect. The majority of waits could turn their hand to almost any instrument if the need arose; they would also have been accomplished singers, whether in Church or in the tavern. Their duties could vary, from welcoming royal visitors, to leading mayoral processions on civic occasions, or playing through the town streets, to wake the townsfolk on dark winter mornings. The waits were salaried, uniformed and liveried, with silver chains of office, bearing the town's coat of arms. Waits were usually bound by the restrictive rules of the Musicians' Guild, which tended to limit the scope of their activities to within their own town boundaries. In some towns, they needed a special licence if they were to play outside the town walls. The waits survived until 1835, when their abolition under the Municipal Reform Act led to the formation of brass bands. Many of the surviving musicians become founder band members.

The need for musical accompaniment in religious services continued after 1644, when the Puritans decreed that all church organs were to be removed. This gave instrumentalists and vocalists the opportunity to perform regularly in church. On the other hand, there was a puritanical dislike of music in church, which, unfortunately, didn't support their position. Thankfully, the survival and cultivation of music was assured, owing much to the leaders of society, royalty and Church leaders. Independently, local people were being taught by the itinerant professional musicians to play various instruments. Those parishes that recognised the need for musical accompaniment in religious service constructed elevated wooden galleries within churches as a platform for the musicians. Church bands, often groups of six musicians, became popular. The new galleries were generally installed behind the congregation, with the musicians facing the altar. From the 19th century onwards, following the developing preferences for harmoniums and American organs to bands, many galleries were removed. Thankfully, one local example of a musicians' gallery survives in Llanbister Church, along with remnants of the instruments used there. Due to the limited availability of musical instruments, players would perform on what was available. They would not necessarily be able to read music; and the resulting sounds and tuning would be a combination of what best could be achieved. The improvising ability of musicians in Wales, especially that which was associated with the itinerant instrumentalists, can be seen in relation to the emergence of published music and its effect on Welsh traditional music in the 18th century.

Music History

A drawing by Reverend Edwards (1829) depicts a group of three musicians playing within the grounds of Aberystwyth Castle. The date of the drawing supports the possibility that the players are members of the waits, although their solitary duty is witnessed by just one person. Collection: NLW Drawing, volume 404, page 24

Aber Prom

This modern form of musical entertainment would have relied upon a development of needs, which included music as part of a growing social order. There had been a tradition of preserving oral music, well before it was put on paper; its survival credited to those able to pass on their skills in the continuity of performing publicly. By the 19th century, successions of composers took advantage of the music publishing scene, to meet the increasingly popular need for song and anthem. The first brass bands in Wales were formed between 1816 and 1818. The first was probably in the Gwent town of Blaina. Another of the pioneer bands was formed by the Ironmaster of Cyfartha, near Merthyr Tydfil, Robert Crawshay, in 1838. He provided work at his ironworks for players and, consequently, formed a band of thirty musicians.

He brought his family to Aberystwyth for a fortnight's holiday in the summers of the 1870s, along with his entire brass band, which would provide free musical entertainment for the visitors on the promenade. The inhabitants and visitors collected £300 for the band, but, at Mr Crawshay's request, all the money was returned to the donors. The museum at Cyfartha Castle displays examples of the band's original instruments. A typical example of band instruments in 1840 would have included cornet, trumpet, trombone, clarinet, flute, ophicleide, cornopean and assorted drums.

By the 1820s, the more discerning members of the public demanded a place to listen to fine music, rather than the limited outpourings of the seasonal performer. The lack of a purpose built concert hall, capable of hosting orchestral concerts, encouraged them to contribute to the building of a suitable place. £2,000 was raised, and the Assembly Rooms, in a classic Georgian style, were built in Laura Place. The design is credited to George Repton, the son of Humphrey Repton, a partner of the famous architect John Nash. The people of Aberystwyth were now able to meet and enjoy musical concerts in comfort, and attend grand balls and socialise in splendid surroundings.

A report in the local news column of the *Aberystwyth Observer* of August 7th, 1858 stated: '*A ball took place at the Assembly rooms on Monday evening last under the patronage of Captain Pryse M.P., the Lord Lieutenant of the County. The company commenced to assemble at 10 o'clock and dancing was kept up with great spirit till early dawn.*'

The assembly rooms attracted many orchestral players into the town, in the early years. Within fifty years of opening, it was hosting a wider form of entertainment that included vaudeville and music hall variety acts. Travelling entertainers from abroad, who were often introduced by entrepreneurial agents, gave performances of a level that invited criticism in the local press: '*The female troupe of Ethiopian minstrels gave an entertainment at the assembly rooms. The room was well filled, but the performances were not of the most satisfactory character. The entertainment was reproduced on Saturday evening, but judging by the greatly diminished*

Music History

attendance, the audience of the previous evening had not given the best colour to the performance.' (Cambrian News, 12. 3.1870)

The increasing number of mid-Victorian visitors enticed a greater variation of entertainment to the town, although, by the 1840s, while small bands were being invited to play, an uncontrolled situation developed that allowed in an uninvited number of itinerant performers, especially onto the beaches. The consequent quality of performance and the type of musical performance offered became strictly monitored, with an increasing level of control placed by the town council upon promenade entertainment. This was to have a lasting effect on the character of the town as a resort to the present day.

STREET ENTERTAINMENT

Street entertainment became an essential part of the busy town scene and would include a variety of acts such as acrobats, jugglers and musicians. Their main function would be to perform for the passing crowds during Market days, often from a small dais near the Market Hall, at the top end of Great Darkgate Street. This was the main area of town activity for several centuries, until the 1930s.

A 1797 market day street scene in Aberystwyth, depicting live entertainment in front of a large crowd in the vicinity of the Angel Hotel, in Upper Great Darkgate. A platform has been erected outside the hostelry, on which a singer, acrobat, dancer and an accompanying harpist are performing, watched by a large crowd. Collection: Ceredigion Museum

BANDS
BAND ENTERTAINMENT DURING THE VICTORIAN PERIOD

The dissolution of the waits in the 1830s, during the reign of William IV, secured the future of bands, which began to appear at Aberystwyth in the early 1840s. Their emergence coincided with the developing need for entertainment in the pioneering years of tourism in the town and, consequently, as in other resorts, bands became the principal form of promenade entertainment. Across the United Kingdom, the general public progressively regarded the developing coastal towns as places to visit and hear this form of music publicly, in the knowledge that they could get there reasonably cheaply by public transport. Before the luxury of the motor car, the train to the seaside became the norm. Local residents and long stay visitors may have had a different opinion about the annual influx of trippers, as they become known, and the associated lively level of entertainment provided for them.

Charles Dickens often stayed at Broadstairs, on the Kent coast and, in 1847, whilst attempting to write, he complained: *'Unless it pours with rain I cannot write half an hour without the most excruciating Organs, Fiddles or Gleemen.'*

Aberystwyth, in line with other resorts across the country, met with an equal clamour for the seaside, becoming inundated with all types of itinerant entertainers, keen to take advantage of those who associated their trip to the coast with the provision of entertainment. From those early pioneering days in the 19th century, the type and amount of live outdoor entertainment became tightly monitored by the controlling Borough Council. The time, location and type of performance had to be vetted annually; all applications to provide entertainment publicly had to be made to them. Many were refused permission to set up a performing 'pitch' anywhere. It was made clear to all that the choice of band, pierrot troupe, minstrel group and other forms of beach performance was solely the council's annual decision. Their bold direction shaped the resort from those pioneering days to the present. Those early local decisions provided a level of entertainment that visitors welcomed. The appeal achieved was aimed, not necessarily at the casual visitor, but at those who might have wished to return the following year.

From the early part of the 19th century up to the 1890s, it was usual to hire bands from outside the vicinity. One such was a group of German brass players, in 1847, conducted by Phillipe Kurz. Their musical ability appealed to the residents and visitors, and they were hired to play for several summer seasons to follow. In 1846, the King of Saxony visited the town unofficially, but his presence was soon discovered and led to a gathering of people and musicians outside his lodgings, *'… with such music as the place could afford.'* (Carus, Carl Gustav, The King of Saxony's Journey through England and Scotland in the year 1844)

This c. 1860 German band of musicians on Marine Terrace are uniformly dressed with peaked caps, suggesting a formal group of five, playing instruments that include ophicleides, cornets and a horn. Photographer unknown.

Collection: National Library of Wales

Aber Prom

As the reader of the diary noted, the music was probably performed by: *'His own incompatible Germans,'* since many bands at that time were of German origin.

In the 1850s, Jacob Leon, a long established jeweller and silversmith of Pier Street, took over the baton of the summer band. He also held a position of authority within the borough as a Town Improvement Commissioner.

The earliest known photograph of promenade entertainment at Aberystwyth includes a band of five musicians standing on Marine Terrace, about 1860. It is likely that it is the German band that often played in the town from the 1840s. By 1854, the entertainment they provided provoked the statement: *'Aberystwyth had an efficient public band.'* Cliffe, C.F., (1854), *'The book of South Wales, the Bristol Channel, Monmouthshire and the Wye'*.

The ophicleide was virtually extinct by this time, along with the serpent, a similar type of instrument. The ophicleide was introduced by Jean Hilaire Aste in 1821, and had a keyed barrel similar to a clarinet, but with a circular wooden mouthpiece, similar to today's brass shape. It would generally be used to play the bass part, although it was capable of being played as a solo instrument. Its name was derived from the Greek word *'Ophis'* for serpent and *'Klies'* for closing. George Bernard Shaw, the Irish playwright, once described the instrument as a *'Chromatic bullock.'*

An advert in the *Aberystwyth Observer*, which ran for several summer weeks during July 1859, proclaimed:

> **THE BAND**
> USUALLY PERFORMING AT ABERYSTWYTH DURING THE SEASON BEG TO INFORM THE VISITING GENTRY THAT BEING DEPENDENT FOR SUPPORT UPON VOLUNTARY CONTRIBUTIONS THEY WILL FEEL GRATEFUL FOR THEIR KIND ASSISTANCE WHICH THEY MOST RESPECTFULLY SOLICIT.
> **BALLS, QUADRILLE PARTIES AND CONCERTS**
> ATTENDED IN TOWN AND COUNTRY
> **PHILLIPE KURZ – LEADER**

It is apparent that financial support, later guaranteed by contract with the local authorities, had not been established at that time. This does not suggest that their arrival went unappreciated, at least not by the local press: *'The present fine weather, we are happy to say has been the means of drawing an increased number of visitors to our town, for the purpose of receiving the benefit of its invigorating breezes and refreshing waters. It gives us great pleasure also to state that the excellent German band which, under the able leadership of Herr Phillipe Kurz has so often enlivened our town during past seasons, has again arrived amongst us, and we trust that they will not only meet with due appreciation of their merits as musicians, but with that encouragement which they so truly deserve.'* Aberystwyth Observer, Saturday, 14. 7. 1860

For the last two decades of the 19th century, a performing licence would be granted to the promenade band selected to play for the season. They would be paid a regular wage, on the understanding that they were not to collect gratuities from the public.

Earlier, in July 1869, the dissatisfaction between those willing to provide entertainment and the lack of an established financial arrangement with the local authorities was exemplified in an advert placed by the town band in the local press, pleading for support during the summer season.

The *Aberystwyth Observer* advertised on July 24th, 1869 the following:

> TOWN BAND
> ENTIRELY SUPPORTED BY VOLUNTARY CONTRIBUTIONS
> THE PUBLIC ARE RESPECTFULLY INFORMED THAT THE TOWN BAND WILL PLAY ON VARIOUS PARTS OF THE
> MARINE TERRACE
> FROM 9 – 11 A.M.
> AND
> 5.30 – 7.30P.M.
> AND ON
> THE PROMENADE PIER
> FROM 11.30 – 12.30P.M.
> AND 8 – 9P.M. DAILY
> THE ADMISSION TO THE PIER PERFORMANCE
> WILL BE TWOPENCE
> THE ADDITIONAL ONE PENNY
> BEING FOR THE BENEFIT OF THE BAND
> T. DUNCANSON BANDMASTER

These must have been remarkably long days for the performers and also the band librarian, who would have been heavily relied upon to produce a sufficiently extensive repertoire to overcome any noticeable repetition of music.

By 1875, the town could boast the existence of more than five bands during the summer months. They would have included the local militia band, the Briton, the Excelsior, the Pier, two family bands and the Salvation Army 'Drum and Yell' band. Obviously, the first four would have been bands that relied on local players to support their existence at times of engagement. They would not necessarily have been regularly practising bands. There was great rivalry between two: both vying for the lucrative summer engagement on the promenade, which meant seasonal work for up to fifteen men for the season. The Excelsior band continued in existence until the turn of the century, when it appears it merged with the Briton band to become The Town Band. It is assumed that the Pier band, which included imported seasonal players and locals, would not have been involved in commitments other than those on the pier. The promenade band was considered as the prime provider of outside public entertainment, and they would have been the sole band hired during a particular year. During the year of 1875, the amateur band of the Rowland family was hired as the promenade band to play throughout the season.

The Salvation Army band could have been a locally arranged group that consisted of followers of the cause, who would voluntarily play available instruments such as tambourines and drums to accompany singing. They wouldn't necessarily have been part of the regular entertainment scene, other than creating an attraction on the beach or promenade for those wishing to share in their cause.

The Briton Band

This band was supported by a local philanthropic industrialist, who owned the Briton Slate Works in upper Cambrian Street. It was run by John Morris, who described himself as an *'enamelled slate manufacturer employing ten men and five boys.'* He was joined in partnership in 1880 by Councillor Peter Jones, a prominent figure in Aberystwyth, and Mayor in 1879-80. The Briton Band performed regularly in the town for about thirty years, from the early 1890s. During its existence, it had the use of a mobile bandstand, which could be moved about the town and could be used after dark. It was fitted with gas lamps, which were connected to convenient mains outlets in the town, in particular, on the promenade. In October 1890, the police court in Aberystwyth fined a number of youths for sending the movable bandstand, with themselves upon it, against the railings on Marine Terrace. *'That some of the youths were not killed is a marvel, they pushed the cumbersome thing onto the road leading to Bryn y Mor and then allowed it to go down the hill towards the sea. There was a very heavy sea that night and the lower portion of the Parade was crowded with people watching the waves rising above the wall.'* (Cambrian News, 17.10. 1890)

The Excelsior Band

It hasn't been established whether the name of the Excelsior Band is derived from the name of a local industry, or in association with a local football team of the same name: the *Excelsiors*. All the same, the well known, local 23 brass-instrument players were led by Jack Edwards (1853-1942), a well-respected businessman and music tutor, who had been appointed as the first brass tutor at the University Music Department by Sir Walford Davies, Professor and Head of Music.

The leaders of both these bands played in other groups. In November 1890, the *Cambrian News* reported: *'The Aberystwyth Orchestral Society gave a concert in the Assembly rooms. Members of the Orchestra included J T Rees, Clarinet; J H Rowe and Jack Edward, Cornets; and E Rowe, Trombone. Mr Rowe, the Solo Cornet player was encored for performing a great many quavers in remarkably quick time.'*

A few months later, in January 1891, J H Rowe was one of four brothers who transferred from the Excelsior band to the Briton band, due to a disagreement. He became the conductor of the Town Band from 1892 to 1918 and also became the town's Musical Director. (*Cambrian News* 16.1.1891)

Despite attempts to control the number of performances, there were conflicts between the bands and the minstrels. In 1891, the Briton and Excelsior bands had both been playing selections on the promenade, causing a correspondent to write to the *Cambrian News*, suggesting that: *'The big drums should*

The Briton Band pose for the photographer on Aberystwyth beach, below the promenade bandstand, c. 1890s, with their conductor, J H Rowe. Photographer unknown. Collection: Peter Henley

The Excelsior band with their conductor, Jack Edwards c. 1890s. Collection: Peter Henley, Photographer: Arthur Lewis

not be played, or at least but sparingly, as the continuous thud can be heard a longer distance than the instruments, and not only causes annoyance but disturbs the band on the pier and the minstrel troupes.' (Cambrian News, 17.7.1891)

The Aberystwyth Improvement Company Band

The Pier Company Band and Orchestra appears to have been formed in about 1894 and continued in existence until the first years of the 20th century. It was established by the Aberystwyth Improvement Company to perform on the newly reconstructed Pier, with its pavilion at one end and bandstand at the other. The band was engaged before the pier was complete, so they performed on a temporary bandstand on the beach, which became the subject of complaints by the Corporation. The Corporation could control who performed on the terrace and the castle, but had no control over performances on the pier, which was privately owned. Nor could they control the membership of the Town Band, so when T B Grant decided *to engage a magnificent band, such a one as Aberystwyth had not before had in the town,'* The Corporation were not in a position to stop members of the Town Band joining it, or to offer more money to them if the pay was better than theirs. It appears that the Corporation were forced to negotiate with the Pier Company for the joint engagement of a band for 1896, the year the new Pavilion was to be opened, to avoid competition. (*Cambrian News* 2. 2.1894 and 28.1.1896).

The Tyler Family Band

There were also several small family bands that performed in Aberystwyth. The Tylers' band was conducted by the head of the family, George H Tyler, who obviously led a busy life, conducting both his own band and the Aberystwyth Promenade Band during the 1870s, and performing regularly on the Pier in 1872-3, just after it was re-opened. A complimentary article in the *Aberystwyth Observer* in 1873 included some heartfelt and philosophizing editorial comments about the day: *'The performances of the Tyler band are giving great satisfaction at the concerts in aid of the subsidy of the Band committee; as from the favourable acoustic properties of the charming concert room at the Queen's Hotel, the melodious tones of the silver instruments of the bands are heard with delicate distinctness, however pianissimo the points may be rendered. A lesson in social life is imparted by the appearance and heartfelt action of the members of this well-conducted Family band. Harmony in life and harmony in tone, must impress itself favourably; and the particular bearing of this bond of unity and of unison should teach us all the value of inculcating art or other general studies for the young, as against the life of idleness we too frequently see around us.'*

The Rowland Family band

The Rowland Family band, another 1870s, local musical family band, consisted of eight players, the father and seven sons. They originated from a military background and had played in the band of her Majesty's 4th King's Own Royal Regiment. They

The Pier Company Band and Orchestra was conducted by Mr J H Rowe of Aberystwyth during the initial years of the 20th century, while the scheduling of musical events on the Pier was controlled by the Aberystwyth Improvement Company. The photograph, c. 1900, was taken on the pier and depicts their wind band of 19 players, who were mostly imported for the summer months.

Collection: NLW. Photographer: Arthur Lewis

Aber Prom

ABERYSTWYTH
TOWN BAND FUND.
SEASON 1875.

THE
Queen's Hotel Assembly Room.

THE TWELFTH
Evening Concert
OF
VOCAL & INSTRUMENTAL MUSIC,
BY SEVERAL
LADIES AND GENTLEMEN AMATEURS,
AND BY THE
BAND OF THE
ROWLAND FAMILY,
(Mr. Rowland and his Seven Sons)

Who will appear in their splendid new Troubadour Costumes, as worn by the Ancient Troubadours of the time of Charles II.

On Wednesday, September 8th, 1875,
To commence at Half-past 8 o'clock.

ADMISSION—Front Seats, 2s., and by Season Family Tickets; Second Seats, 1s.

To be had at the Hotels, and at Messrs. J. Morgan's (late Cox's) Library, and J. Evans', Music Warehouse, Pier Street.

J. MORGAN (LATE J. COX), MACHINE PRINTER, PIER STREET, ABERYSTWYTH.

The Rowland family band concert programme, 1875. Collection: Peter Henley

had previously served as a string band to the Queen's Royal Balmoral minstrels. Locally, they were often hired to provide seasonal entertainment, from 1875, dressed in troubadour costumes of the style prevalent during the reign of King Charles II. Their other duties included providing string and brass formations for the promenade bandstand.

The people of late Victorian Britain became more interested in light entertainment than the healthy pursuits and formal social events that their predecessors in the early years of the 19th century had enjoyed. Until the 1890s, bands performed for them but only with the consent of the local Corporation. In the spring of most years, the Corporation advertised for bands and other entertainers to perform during the season, which ran from May to September, and drew up a contract of how many performers were to play, where they were to perform and how often. Previously, in 1873, the Corporation had decided to establish a committee to superintend the musical arrangements of a public band.

Councillors keenly reported any infringements of these regulations and made suggestions. For example: in 1879, a plebiscite of local people, concerned about the way street entertainment was organised, subtly raised the matter of its effect upon those living nearby: *'It has been suggested by several of the Aberystwyth ratepayers and Councilmen, that if the band was to play half an hour less in the morning and go to the castle grounds to play from three to four in the afternoon, it would be a great acquisition to the Bandsmen, and also would amuse the visitors and excursionists.'* (*Cambrian News* 10.1.1879)

Not all were in favour of repositioning the band from the built up areas to the remoteness of the castle grounds. A letter was received from Mr W R Hall, complaining that the town band had only played in Victoria Terrace once during the past six weeks. It was resolved that the complaint, together with the question of playing in other parts of the town and the hours during which the band play, be referred to the General Purposes Committee for consideration and report. As a result, it was proposed in council: *'That instruction is given to the band confining their performances to the Marine Terrace and Victoria Terrace during the remainder of the season, and that they play until 9.30 p.m. each evening. Also that instruction is given that in case of interruption through rain compelling the band to cease playing at the appointed places that they start playing on the following evenings at the place they left off.'* (*Cambrian News*, 20.8.1895)

In 1880, an advert for a summer band at Aberystwyth resulted in *'forty to fifty'* applications. The Corporation Band committee selected the Theatre Royal Band from Great Grimsby, who had previously played at Margate and other watering places. It consisted of two violinists, piccolo, flute, harp, double bass, cornet, clarinet, trombone, a sentimental vocalist and a business manager. (*Cambrian News*, 20.5.1880)

During the mid 1880s, Thomas Handley provided a band for the season, but, in 1887, it was proposed: *'That no band for the season be provided this season due to the lack of interest by lodging house keepers, but Sergeant Kain, the late Bandmaster's application*

Aber Prom

to provide a band be granted.' Sergeant Kain was the Bandmaster of the local Militia band, based in the Barracks on Penglais. It was later reported that there were not enough performances and one song was objectionable. (Aberystwyth Town Council minutes, 19th April 1887, Ceredigion Archives)

Obviously, by this time, a level of disagreement was developing between the Corporation Entertainment Committee and the local hoteliers regarding the type and quality of promenade entertainment. The following year, in 1888, there was a proposal to call a meeting of the ratepayers, to discuss the corporation subscribing a sum of money to secure the engagement of a thoroughly efficient band, but this was clearly a failure, since two weeks later, the Corporation decided to take no steps to procure a band, again, *'owing to the indifference of the lodging house keepers.'* (Aberystwyth Town Council minutes, 21st January 1888, Ceredigion Archives)

A level of contractual disassociation from a previous annual commitment to provide and hire a summer band developed with an open invitation from the Town Clerk to Mr Barnett, a Bandmaster, to bring his band to the town, stating that the Town Council do not intend engaging a band for the season of 1888. (*Cambrian News*, 1.5.1888)

By 1890, the Council was writing: *'Your committee having been in correspondence with the Aberystwyth Pier Company and also with Mr Dyson, are unanimously of the Opinion that it is desirable to accept the proposal made by Mr Dyson to provide during the season a 1st class musical entertainment subject to the details of engagement and other matters being approved by the Council.'* (*Cambrian News*, 20.5. 1890 NLW)

Not all comments were critical, for example, in 1890, it was reported: *'Mr De La Rue Lloyd has been engaged as the comic singer on the pier. His selection appears to include songs full of real fun and not a catalogue of equivocal rubbish.'* (*Cambrian News*, 8. 8. 1890)

By 1890, the Mayor, Councillor William Henry Palmer, proprietor of the Belle Vue and Queen's Hotel, was still keen to hire minstrels from away; although he felt that there should be a tighter control on the type of entertainment provided on the promenade. The Council made bye-laws to stop itinerants freely appointing themselves a pitch on the beach, and were keen to reduce the number of bands performing. The Mayor urged his council: *'The Council band committee thought it desirable to employ local bands until the minstrels came and possibly after they left. It was said that the Visitors complained that the town was dull and would probably leave or not prolong their stay unless entertainment was provided. Mr Palmer hoped the Council would vote in support of local talent and that the young men of the town would combine in providing a first rate band which would be a credit to the town. They would make themselves proficient by practising throughout the winter months and if the council paid them reasonably for their services in the summer months it would be something for them to look forward to. Moreover, the town would have a respectable band and not a lot of drunken men who played just when and how they liked with little variation of tunes. He would not mind voting £100 to a good band of local performers.'* (*Cambrian News*, 4. 6. 1880)

Previously, the hiring of entertainers from away had often turned out to be costly and occasionally unsatisfactory, although, during the previous summer, the main provider of promenade entertainment was one of the local bands. It was established that: '…*last summer the Briton band was popular with visitors, and night after night in attracting larger crowds than were ever attracted by a band before.*' (*Cambrian News*, August 1892)

On the 7th July, 1891, the Corporation agreed to set aside £120 to engage the services of local bands (Town Council Minutes, 7.12.1891) but they decided that they would appoint only one - the Briton Band. It was felt that: '*If the council had given the other band* (The Excelsior) *a chance, as was desired by some members, the element of permanence which is so essential to success would have been lacking. A musical nucleus has now been formed and it is for the musicians of the town and district. There is no reason why Aberystwyth should not become as celebrated for its brass band as for its other great attractions and advantages.*' (*Cambrian News*, 15.12.1891)

The Briton Band was engaged for the 1892 season. They were to play three days a week on the Marine and Victoria Terraces, with at least fifteen performers in the evenings, for two hours, and eight performers on the alternate mornings, also for two hours. Since the Corporation were paying them £29/14/0 per month, they were not allowed to solicit subscriptions or donations from the audience. (*Cambrian News*, 1.4. 1892; Town Council Minutes 4.4.1892)

Meanwhile, the downtrodden Excelsior band continued to apply for the position of Town Band, but the Briton band was selected each year as criticism continued: '*There will always be the fastidious critic who cannot be satisfied: the general public are not hard to please if honest attempts are made with average skill to please them.*' (*Cambrian News*, 16. 12. 1892)

In 1899, Mr J H Rowe, formerly of the Briton band, became conductor of the Pier Company band. (*Cambrian News* 11.12.1899) In 1911, he was appointed manager of municipal entertainment in the town, probably the first person to receive this appointment. Most British bands had modelled themselves on a standard playing configuration. Wind groups that had survived until this period succumbed to the success of the popular brass band. The decline and disappearance of the pioneering German bands from the British resorts became apparent. By 1914, they were nowhere to be found on our shores. A refrain set to a popular tune circulated the British music halls.

'Has anyone seen a *German* band?
German band
German band
I've looked everywhere both near and far,
Near and far
Ja, Ja, Ja
But I miss my Fritz
What plays twiddley-bits
On the big Trombone'
(Extract from 'Beside the Seaside' by James Walvin. 1978)

Aber Prom

CARDIGAN MILITIA BAND

The Cardigan Militia was formed in 1762 and existed under various names until the end of the Great War (1914-1918). The earliest record of their existence is from an article of 1801, stating that they were observed marching to the beat of a drum. (Martyn, 1801) Their role was primarily as a military presence locally, but their appearance on the promenade was recorded both in the capacity of a military force and as a source of entertainment during the summer. Frequent applications were made by their commanding officer for permission to play on the terrace. In 1824, the local guide book reported that: '*The promenade is occasionally enlivened by a small military band belonging to the county regiment,*' and that: '*on alternate Fridays during the season, a small military band played in the assembly rooms.*' (Pritchard, T J Ll (1824), *The New Aberystwyth Guide*, pp.9, 17)

The Cardigan Militia Volunteers were formed around 1860 and were based in the 1867-built barracks on Penglais Hill (now replaced by Maes Gogerddan flats). The Volunteers soon formed a military band under the baton of its conductor, Sergeant Kain (or Cain). It relied principally upon the musical abilities of bandsmen drawn from the ranks of local bands, who joined the Volunteers and wore the uniform of the Royal Cardigan Militia.

The band was called upon to lead the parades of volunteers, when they were in Aberystwyth for training. They would have used the flat Northern approach road into the town to practise their marching, hence its name: North Parade. The militia band continued to play a prominent role in providing musical entertainment locally, especially on the promenade and castle, for a period of about sixty years, from 1860.

The band of the Royal Cardigan Militia in 1877. In its smart military uniform, this volunteer band, based at Gogerddan Barracks, near Penglais Terrace, appeared regularly on the promenade terraces, having drawn its players from local sources. One surname amongst others that became synonymous with banding locally was Warrington. Several generations of the family played in all the local bands over a period of 130 years.

Collection: Peter Henley

Music History

Royal Cardiganshire Militia Band, 43 Years Ago.

Top Row.—William Morgan, Richard Jenkins, Richard Lewis, John Jones, Griffith Jones, James Allen.
Second Row.—William Jeffries, David Morgan, William Warrington, Bandmaster Cain, William James, Meciah Warrington, William Berry.
Third Row.—Davies Jones, Thomas Davies (Drummer), Cpl. David Morgan, George Berry, George Foster, and Thomas Berry.
From Photo lent by Mr. W. Warrington, Terrace Road.

Cambrian News: June 25th 1920

The Royal Cardigan Militia Band marching along Marine Terrace c. 1905. This area, known as 'The Terrace', hadn't succumbed yet to high levels of traffic and was a popular spot for daily entertainment.

Collection: Peter Henley, Publisher: J & J Gibson, 'The *Cambrian News*'

Music History

A postcard from Aberystwyth, posted on August 21st, 1915
'The band is grand at Aberystwyth.'

Collection: Ann Lucas

ABERYSTWYTH SILVER BAND

Within a few years, following the end of the First World War, a revival of interest in *'a trip to the coast'* was inevitable. The combination of an established rail network and roads with increasingly reliable motor cars and coaches allowed the excursionists to flock to the coast in millions. Seaside resorts geared themselves up to meet the resurgence of interest leading into the 1920s. The style of entertainment locally was encouraged into the era of the concert party, albeit at a humbler level, in the Coliseum and Pier pavilion. The promenade entertainment still relied upon the local band, which responded to the public's continuing interest in traditional seaside entertainment. By 1922, the town band, numbering eighteen, was employed to play each evening for two hours, except Sunday, during the peak holiday months, for £35 per week, in the old bandstand on the promenade. Out of this amount, the band would pay for the services of two professional players, usually a solo cornet or euphonium player, very often from the town band at Gwaun Cae Gurwen, in south Wales. One of the players was very tall and easily recognisable, and he was known affectionately as *'Tal'* Morris.

Until 1926, difficulties in finding a suitable rehearsal room for use throughout the winter had not been overcome. The shared use of the skating rink in Queen's Square (which stood on the green adjacent to today's Morfa Chapel), and its proximity to dwelling houses made it continually unpractical.

The people of the town and the borough council, who controlled the band, had, by 1926, come to the decision that the band should have its own band hall. A decision was made to build on an open site in Smithfield, now known as the Ystwyth Retail Park. In 2001, the band celebrated the 75th anniversary of the band hall's existence. To coincide with the use of the new band room, the people of the town collected sufficient money by public subscription to purchase a completely new set of silver plated instruments.

The band, with its overwhelming local support, continued its role in local entertainment and civic duty through the next decade and up until the onset of war in 1939. One interesting occurrence during the 1930s was the joint conductorship of the Aberystwyth Municipal Orchestra and the Aberystwyth Silver Band by G Stephen Evans ARCO, MRST, who, for a short period, shared the bandmaster's role with Cornelius (Connie) C Richardes of Penglais Mansion, which later became the University Vice Chancellor's residence. Several of the regular players had played for the town band for over forty years, one in particular, who had played the same type of instrument, an E *flat* tenor horn, for the period 1895-1935, was the well known beach photographer, William Jenkins, known locally as Will Nell. Another who served for that period was Ned Lewis, brother of Arthur Lewis, the well known local photographer. He played drums for most of the bands that existed in Aberystwyth from the turn of the 20th century and into the mid 1930s. His son Philip became a musician with the Ralph Davies dance band on B *flat* trombone and, later, guitar.

The Aberystwyth Silver Band had recruited many new young players by 1935, bringing their playing membership up to twenty-four. The expansion may have coincided with the holding of the Welsh Brass Band Championship in the castle grounds the previous year. Their conductor was Haydn Lewis, brother of the Promenade Orchestra leader, Logan Lewis. The solo cornet player was Charles Ansley and the euphonium player Cornelius Richardes.

ABERYSTWYTH BRITISH LEGION SILVER BAND – POST WWII

Following the commencement of World War Two hostilities in 1939, the town band was asked to hand in its instruments to the borough council for wartime storage. The bandmaster, Charles Ansley, was asked to carry out the formal task, and the instruments were subsequently placed under a tarpaulin in a corner of a council yard in Park Avenue, until 1945. The now empty Park Avenue band room was requisitioned by the Home Guard and the National Fire Service for the duration of the war. Surprisingly, several attempts were made by the armed forces and the British Legion to acquire the instruments for their use. The owners and guardians of the instruments, the Town Council, considered the applications and promptly turned them down.

By 1948, the returning servicemen, keen to re-establish the band, were given the opportunity to re-occupy the original band room and reclaim the instruments from storage.

Although the band had been exclusively brass for many years before the war, woodwind instruments that had been in its possession from a previous era had also been included in the hand-over and, sadly, didn't survive the elements and were abandoned. The band from that time has maintained the nationally established brass band formation.

Aberystwyth British Legion Band Silver Band.
By 1950, the newly established British Legion band, under the baton of William Dickie, was invited to play at many venues within the town, including a garden performance at the former residential home at Bronglais, which stood on the site of today's Hospital car park. Led by Roy Ansley, the cornet players include David Lewis, Wyndham Davies, Hywel Jones and Donald Warrington.

Collection: Peter Henley

ABERYSTWYTH AND DISTRICT SILVER BAND. By 1976, the appointed bandmaster was Leonard (Bill) James, originally from Aberdare. He lectured at the University Music Department under Professor Parrott, who was Chairman of the band. Leonard James composed two marches, which he dedicated to the band in 1977. He later conducted the band during a visit to Aberystwyth's twin town, St Brieuc, in Brittany, and also to contests on several occasions in north and west Wales. The vocalist in the photograph is Carys Rees Jones. Carys sang with the band on the promenade for several seasons in the 1970s, before becoming a professional singer and television actress.

Left to right back: George Richards, Ian Smith, Gregory Slay, David Henderson, Emyr Jones, Aneurin Hughes, David Russell Hume, David Davies, Myrddin Hughes and Bill Smith

Left to right, seated: Fred Potter, Celia Evans, John P Evans, Leonard James, Donald Warrington, John R Davies, Bill Dickie, Valerie Edwards, and Peter Henley.

Front row: Helen Rudeforth, Peers Goodman, Geraint Evans and Peter Rudeforth. Collection & Photography: Peter Henley

Music History

By 1949, in an affiliation with the British Legion, the band re-emerged in a new, blue, pseudo military style uniform and appointed Charles Buck from London as Bandmaster, and William Dickie, a Scot, as deputy. Several ex-serving bandsmen filled its ranks, elevating the band to success in the North Wales brass band contest in Rhyl in 1955, with a win and cup in the march section. The association with the British Legion ended in October 1957, when the players decided to return to using the title of Aberystwyth Silver Band. Continued success was further guaranteed under the controlling influence of the town council from 1957.

In 2007, the Aberystwyth Silver Band, under the baton of Geraint Evans, relies heavily on university student players, who come from many countries of the world to study at Aberystwyth. Since the Millennium, there have been visiting players from Japan, USA, Canada, Germany and Luxemburg, Lancashire and Yorkshire!

Aberystwyth Silver Band with Bandmaster Richard Crompton, during a break in performance at the Royal B Appeal concert in the Great Hall at Aberystwyth Art Centre in November 2003.
Collection: Peter Henley

MINSTRELS

A newspaper report confirms that minstrels performed publicly in Aberystwyth in 1866 when: *'Mr J Whitworth, Proprietor of the troupe of Christy's minstrels, gave their ludicrous performances in the assembly rooms.'* (*Aberystwyth Observer*, 8. 9. 1866)

It's possible that their performance may have had a British origin, considering that the minstrel style based upon an American development did not enter the country until the 1870s, and was not found locally until the 1890s. The performances of Thomas Dartmouth Rice (1808 – 1860) inspired the introduction of *'nigger minstrels'* in the American South. He was known to all as *'Daddy Thomas Rice'* and was regarded as the first white minstrel man in *'black face'* make-up. He gained success with his rendition of an old, crippled, Cincinnati Afro-American by the name of Jim Crow, who originally sang what was known as a *'Negro Ditty.'*

From 1870, minstrels were performing in his style in many of the major British resorts. In Britain, minstrels, then widely publicised as *'niggers'* or *'white coons'*, painted their faces black, sang sentimental plantation songs, and became known as: *The Kings of the Promenade and the Pier*. (Walvin, J, *Beside the Seaside*, 1978)

From the 1890s, the previous popular entertainment provided solely by the local band at Aberystwyth was challenged with the appearance of the more versatile minstrels. The emergence of Harry Collins and his company and successive troupes transformed the style and projection of promenade entertainment over the following forty years.

HARRY COLLINS

From 1892 the appearance of Harry Collins offered audiences *'Hilarity not vulgarity,'* in his seaside shows at Aberystwyth, with banter, audience participation and clean family entertainment. His *'Merry Mascots'* played a variety of musical instruments that included violin, harp, flute, cornet and, of course, the ever popular tenor banjo, played by Harry Collins himself. They sported costumes that represented a style similar to naval uniform, with officers' dark, double-breasted blazers, white trousers and shoes. Their headwear included peaked, white-topped caps with a nautical badge. To offset the blazers, they wore white shirts with stiffened collars, and a dark tie. Often, several of the party would *'black up'* for their minstrel shows, with two playing the part of navy ratings, with white, wide-brimmed hats and pinafores.

They obviously had backstage several changes of outfit for their daily routine. For the evening concerts within the Pier Pavilion they wore formal evening suits with top hats and bow ties, while the female singer and harpist wore full length white cotton dresses. They performed morning and evening on the promenade, and on the pier in the afternoon, every weekday from Whit Monday until mid September, each year from 1890 to 1911. Towards the end of each season, Harry Collins produced a Benefit Concert in a local hall. In 1899, the concert included

Harry Collins with a troupe of eight entertainers in the pier end open theatre. The men in formal dress and headwear, with the inclusion of a female harpist and a flautist, suggests a different type of performance, although the banjo on Harry Collins' lap does reflect a link with their traditional style of minstrelsy.

Photographer: Arthur Lewis c. 1895. Collection: National Library of Wales

Aber Prom

Harry Collins, the entertainer, and his *'Merry Mascots'* are in the studio of Pickford's Photographer's at 28 Pier Street, c.1900. The backcloth was a popular choice from several available for studio sittings. This particular one was a canvas painting of Constitution Hill, promenade and sea. The *'rocks'* that they were sitting on were made of papier-mâché. Harry Collins provided a troupe of promenade and pier entertainers at Aberystwyth from 1890 -1911.

Collection: Peter Henley

Music History

A Harry Collins poster advertising a Grand Benefit Concert at the Royal Pier Pavilion in 1899. Collection: Ceredigion Museum

a vast range of performances. He described the event as: *'A galaxy of inimitable talent will do their utmost to make this the night of nights and don't you forget it! Oh! What a night we are going to have!'*

Included in the evening's concert were:

Prince Hassan – The wonderful high telephone wire walker

Percy Meye – The wonderful female impersonator and skirt dancer

Beni Zoug Zoug – The funny schoolboy in a novel performance

The Darktown Quartette of comedians in something new

And the new screaming burlesque sketch

(Advertising poster 1899, Ceredigion Museum 180.1)

Like other entertainers, they had to pay a fee to the Town Council with their application for a performance licence. In 1895 this cost £30 for the season. (*Cambrian News* 15. 2. 1896)

By 1900, the summer entertainment troupe, provided by Gilbert Rogers, was being charged £70 for a performing licence, which may be why in that year the Collins minstrels transferred to the privately-owned, open air venue in the bosky surrounds of Elysian Grove on Penglais. They continued to entertain there until at least 1907, although they were in Aberystwyth until 1914.

It is possible that British variety became influenced by the new, 'clean' entertainment that developed in the United States in 1881. Instant success commercially was gained that year, when Tony Pastor, a New York theatre manager, introduced a style of entertainment that was free of vulgarity. It immediately appealed to audiences of all ages and classes. It was further developed as *Vaudeville* by two enterprising showmen, who had previously made a lot of money staging unauthorised productions of Gilbert and Sullivan operas in the United States. The origin of the word is uncertain but is believed to derive from the French slang, '*Voix de Ville*' or 'Songs of the town'. Vaudeville was a determined stand against acts containing blue material, which had '*challenged the Victorian code of sentiment and gentility.'* (Ivan Dee, Chicago 1989). Vaudeville certainly became part of British seaside and music hall entertainment, in many forms that were inoffensive. Its style survived as live entertainment until the 1920s, when moving pictures and radio became more popular.

GILBERT ROGERS

A highly successful and popular minstrel group, the *Merry Minstrel Troopers*, led by Gilbert Rogers, challenged the equally popular Harry Collins for the right to the prestigious promenade contract in 1899, by offering £70 for the privilege. The Rogers troupe appeared annually for a period of five years at Aberystwyth during the final years of the Victorian summers and into the mid Edwardian era. Rogers moved later to Rhyl, where his reformed and re-titled company became the *Gilbert Rogers Jovial Jesters*, from 1907 – 1913. In that later troupe was

Music History

The leader of the Minstrels, Gilbert Rogers, is captured in a snapshot in c.1901, as he approaches the photographer with his money-collecting bag in his right hand, in the act of *bottling*. The seated audience would have paid to sit and watch the minstrels perform, but the opportunity to collect a few extra pennies from those within earshot on the beach nearby wasn't to be missed. He was given permission to erect his striped tent and dais on the beach alongside the bandstand during that year. Source: Ceredigion Museum

Aber Prom

Jack Jewell, father of the famous stage and radio performer Jimmy Jewell. Rogers had performed previously with a well known troupe called *Moore and Burgess*, whose style he brought with him to Aberystwyth; their performances were based on Southern American Negro songs. During his period at Aberystwyth, he regularly alternated his act with a minstrel-style *'black face'* performance, although by 1907 he had abandoned the image and concentrated their appearance on the dress of the emerging *'Concert Party.'*

Surprisingly, Rogers initial application to perform on the castle grounds was rejected, in 1901, by the town council. The initial cautious interest showed allowed them only to erect a portable platform and tent on the beach. (*Cambrian News* 15.3.1901)

Their performing ability obviously overcame any doubt during the period 1901-1904, when they appeared annually in the Pier Pavilion and theatre and in the Constitution Hill pleasure gardens, by arrangement with the controlling Aberystwyth Development Company. The *'black faced'* minstrel troupe, varying in number from eleven to sixteen, appeared flamboyantly dressed in white suits and waistcoats with wide, dark, double piping around the jackets and down the trousers legs, and wore white peaked caps. Their alternative outfits, worn when they were without face paint, included white, double-breasted suits and wide-brimmed, white ribbon hats and white footwear. They regularly performed within the castle grounds, where they erected a simple wooden stage and canvas backdrop and played to small audiences seated on deck-chairs. Four, one hour, daily performances were given: in the morning, afternoon, early and late evening. For the last show, from 9-10 p.m. the performances would be assisted by electrical, or *lime-light*.

Occasionally, when it rained, they would play in a concert room on the top of Constitution Hill, and also for the Aberystwyth Improvement Company on the Pier.

During the winter months, entertainers such as Gilbert Rogers found work at various music halls throughout the country, performing in pantomime in particular. Gilbert Rogers was given a part in *Aladdin* at the Princess Theatre in Bradford in 1903-04. (*Cambrian News* 15. 3. 1901)

A snapshot of Gilbert Rogers flag-waving *Merry Minstrel Troopers* in procession on Marine Terrace, possibly celebrating the relief of Mafeking on May 17th, 1900. They were within a very short distance of the Pier entrance leading to the end theatre, which became a popular venue for them between 1902 and 1907.

Collection: Ceredigion Museum 1994.53.74C. Photographer unknown

The multi-talented Gilbert Rogers minstrel troupe during one of their daily performances at the former pier end theatre at Aberystwyth in 1902, in their distinctive white suits and caps and blacked up faces. Of the fourteen performers on stage, six are playing musical instruments, including at least one brass player on cornet.

Photographer unknown. Collection: Ceredigion Museum

Mr. Gilbert Rogers's Minstrel Troupe, Aberystwyth, 1904.

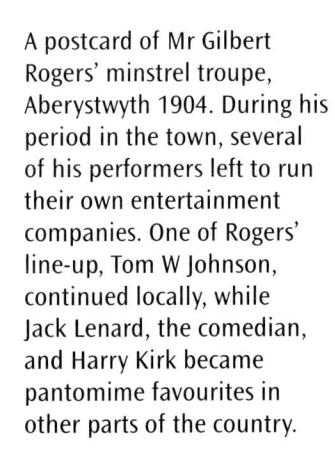

A postcard of Mr Gilbert Rogers' minstrel troupe, Aberystwyth 1904. During his period in the town, several of his performers left to run their own entertainment companies. One of Rogers' line-up, Tom W Johnson, continued locally, while Jack Lenard, the comedian, and Harry Kirk became pantomime favourites in other parts of the country.

Photographer: Knipe and Culliford Collection: Ceredigion Museum AYD10.

As the Gilbert Rogers minstrel troupe sing and dance during their daily summer routine in the castle grounds in 1904, their assistant busies himself to the side of the musicians, sorting music for the following acts. Gilbert Rogers is in the centre of the dancing five, while Harry Kirk sings in front.

Photographer unknown. Collection: Ceredigion Museum

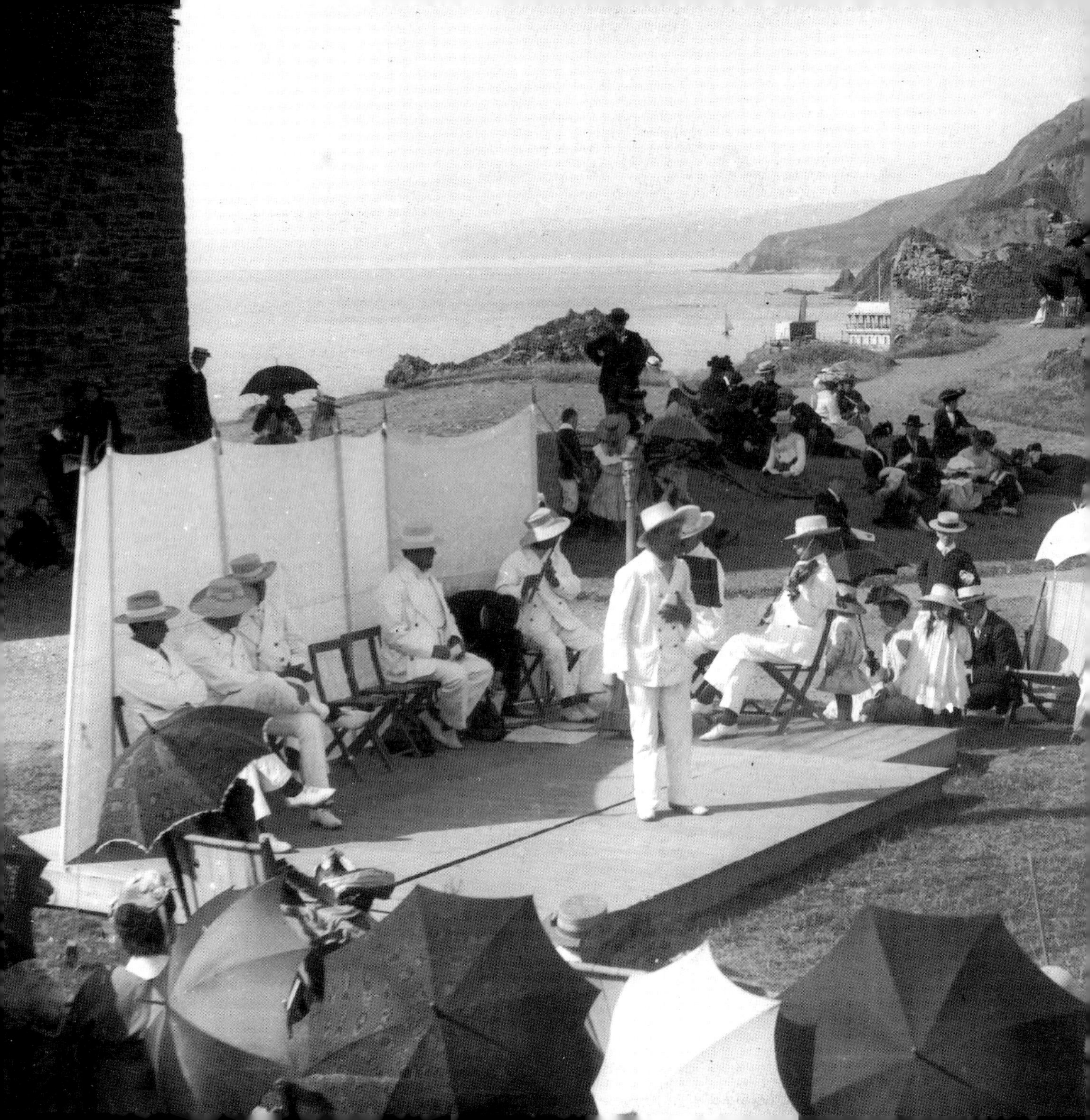

Music History

The Gilbert Rogers troupe is seen entertaining the Edwardian summer visitors in the grounds of Aberystwyth Castle in 1905. They would erect two small wooden stages, one for the performers and another to the side for the musicians, a canvas back-drop and a supply of deck chairs for the audience. Accompanying the entertainment (which would include singing, dancing and comedy) would have been a violinist, flautist and harpist. The flute player doubled also on clarinet.

Photographer: Arthur Lewis
Collection: National Library of Wales

BEACH PERFORMERS
PIERROTS

From the 1890s, the minstrel troupes faced a new and serious challenge to their seaside dominance with the appearance of pierrots. The origins of the pierrots lie in the Italian *Commedia dell'arte troupes* of the mid 17th century. One of its members, Giuseppe Giratoni, joined the Italian company when performing in Paris and subsequently introduced the role and the distinctive costume of the pierrot to France.

They were introduced into Britain in 1891, by Clifford Essex, as a commercial venture, drawing the idea from French pantomime. Following their debut at Henley-on-Thames, Essex completed many summer seasons with his performers at Sandown, on the Isle of Wight. It may have been the fancy dress with its close similarity to that of the circus clown that appealed to the British audience, or perhaps the association with the word 'pier' which led the UK pioneers to take on the name pierrot.

The success of the pierrots sounded the death-knell for other seaside buskers, and by 1904 the popularity of the very successful minstrels had been strongly challenged. The promenaders of the day became attracted to their new style of dress, which seemed to be as decorative as that of any of the performing artists of the period. Their carefully chosen outfits were white cotton, loose-fitting, one-piece suits, or smocks and trousers, ruffled collars and whitened shoes. Sewn to their fronts, arms and legs would be black pom-poms. On their heads they would wear a white pointed, rimmed hat. Their performances were more gentle and refined and they were an instant success. In the major British resorts by the mid 1890s they, rather than the minstrels, had come to characterize beach music and entertainment. They superseded the minstrels like entrepreneurs.

Locally, entertainment was given independently by groups of six to eight performers of pierrots and Negro minstrels. In the early days, they would be accompanied by a strill, a type of portable harmonium, plus a banjo or violin. Bill Neale, a sign writer of New Street, also a cornet player in the local bands, recalled that at peak periods: '*The Pierrots or Minstrels would perform their ditties at one end of the promenade while the band played at the other to avoid any form of disturbance.*'

CATLIN'S PIERROTS

They were founded by Will Catlin, the Scarborough businessman, who took advantage of improving methods of publicity circulation to promote his entertainment business from 1894. He consequently successfully secured the rights to provide pierrot entertainment during the Edwardian summer months at many of the leading holiday resorts in Britain. His original name for the entertainers was '*Favourite Pierrots*', but after performing in front of the Prince of Wales, later to become King Edward VII, at Ruthin Castle, they took on the title *Catlin's Royal Pierrots*, the proud title used to decorate the front of their

A postcard of *Catlin's Royal Pierrots* entertaining the summer visitors at Aberystwyth Castle posted locally on September 8th, 1908. The location is now the putting green and children's playground below the north wall of the castle.

Publisher: ETW Dennis Ltd. Collection: Peter Henley

wooden theatre near the Aberystwyth Castle grounds in 1907-8. They drew large crowds to their daily performances, many paying to sit on the provided chairs encircling the stage, while others would sit on a bank on the site of the former castle barbican. They also performed on temporary stages within the castle grounds, beneath the central tower, and on the beach opposite Marine Terrace.

During a visit by one of His Majesty's warships, they accepted an invitation to perform on board for

A studio photograph of Catlin's Pierrots in Aberystwyth in 1907.

Will Catlin appeared mostly in the north Wales resorts of Rhyl, Llandudno and Colwyn Bay. He was born William Henry Fox, in Leicester, in 1872, and spent his early years at Scarborough, working as a beach entertainer. This was where he formed his own company and introduced pierrot groups into many of the major resorts in the United Kingdom. He died at his home in Llandudno, aged 80, in 1952. The local troupe leader and comedian was Percy Grahame, centre front. The vocalist was Edwin Rose, front left, and the group's ventriloquist, Bobby Edmundson, was second from the right.

Collection: Peter Henley. Photographer unknown

During the initial years of the 20th century, entertainment would have been provided on several sites along Marine Terrace. The pierrot performances of song, dance and banter were often accompanied by black-faced minstrels, playing a harp and violin, attired in straw hats, dark blazers and light trousers, Their shows would have been occasionally interrupted by passing horses and carriages, or by the rare appearance of an early motor car chugging along the Terrace at a site in front of today's Richmond and Helmsman Hotels. Photographer unknown.

Collection: Ceredigion Museum

Aber Prom

During a break in performance on Marine Terrace, around 1900, the summer pierrots jokingly pose for the photographer on an occasion that included another entertainer, who was dressed in a troubadour costume. A young cyclist in typical late Victorian attire includes himself in the photograph, while another stands in the foreground, by a narrow gauge, contractors' track, installed during the construction of the new promenade, south of the pier. The right hand building behind is now Ceredigion, the University student hall of residence.

Collection: Ceredigion Museum. Photographer unknown.

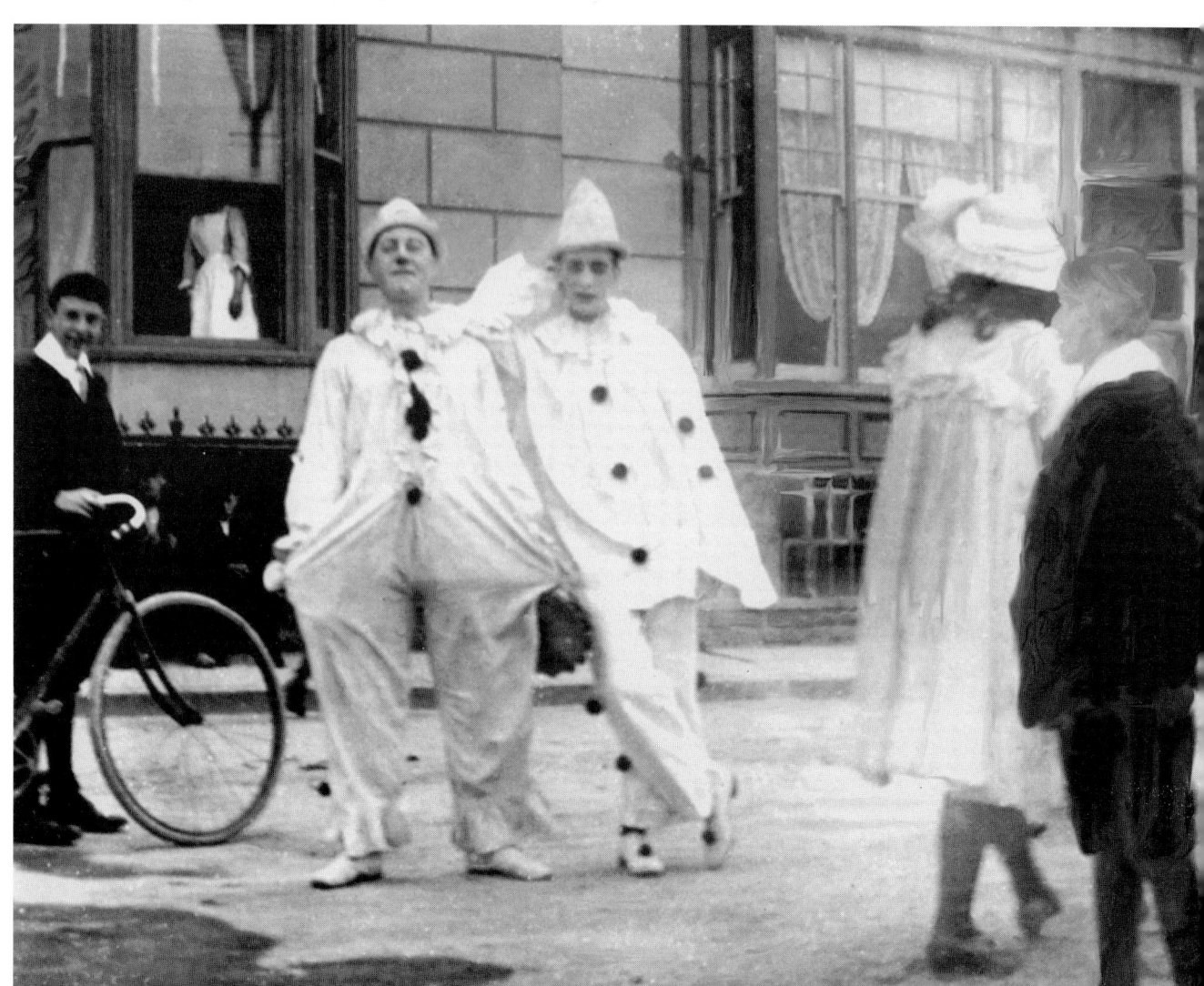

Music History

In their unmistakable pierrot costumes, *Adeler & Sutton's Pierrots* perform on summertime Aberystwyth beach in about 1900. This group of nine would have given three performances daily, on their small beach dais opposite Marine Terrace. Their versatility would have included acts of comedy, singing, dancing and juggling. Accompanying them in their musical performances were instrumentalists playing harmonium, violin and banjo. At the height of their popularity, during the early years of the 20th century, *Adeler & Sutton's Pierrots* were performing at fifteen different resorts around the UK. For many seasons, they were all male. About 1905, their founder, Edwin Adeler, made a popular and successful move to include one lady, a pierrette, in each of his companies nationwide.

Collection: Peter Henley, from Emile Thomas Evans

the Royal Navy Officers and crew. Up to 1914, they were all male performers and were regarded as the *glamour boys* of the day. The smart appearance and manner expected of them inclined towards exemplary rather than dissolute behaviour. They were not allowed to be seen publicly with females, and were also expected to walk from their digs to their pitch in full make-up and costume. All members of the company had to take turns at bottling (collecting money from the audience), using a collecting pouch on the end of a wooden handle. They also sold group postcards and copies of their songs to the public. (Extracts from *Pom-poms and Ruffles* by G.J. Mellor, 1964 and *Promenades and Pierrots* by Bill Pertwee, 1979)

ADELER & SUTTON

During the era of the seaside pierrot, famous named troupes were appearing in many of the British resorts. The beaches and piers of the English east and south coast and a few Welsh beaches were visited by the top names, including the Adeler and Sutton Pierrots. Their name was emblazoned along the sides of Aberystwyth Pier Pavilion at the turn of the 20th century (seen on pages 94-95).

WILL MORRIS

The summer of 1919, following the end of the First World War, was described as the Victory season. The celebration of peace and victory was marked in many ways, especially in song and variety, throughout the nation during that year. The return of the surviving armed forces to their families led to a level of normality and a continuation of work and pleasure. The popularity of the seaside holiday and its associated entertainment was revived. The visitors, the shows, the welcoming hotels and guest houses and full trains became a reality once more. Within ten years, in the mid 1920s, fifteen million people were holidaying in Britain every year. To accommodate this resurgence immediately following the war, new entertainers began appearing at Aberystwyth. Following the successful introduction of pierrots into Britain in the last century, continuing popularity guaranteed their reappearance on the

Will Morris, centre, with his pierrette and pierrot troupe of entertainers in their coloured satin costumes and black skull caps, appeared at Aberystwyth during the 1922 season. Until the appearance of *Uncle Tommy*, in the late 1930s, they may have been the last of the pierrot line of entertainment to perform locally. This beach style of entertainment was becoming dated by the 1920s as the more popular and successful Concert Party era emerged.
Collection: Peter Henley

promenade, pier and Castle in 1919, in the form of *Will Morris's Celebrated Pierrettes and Pierrots*.

They were a formation of nine performers, three women and six men. Included also in their performance was a ventriloquism act by one of the ladies. They all wore distinctive coloured or white traditional pierrot costume with double neck ruffles, and dark pom-poms down their fronts, while the ladies interchanged their outfits with light dresses. Later, in 1924, the men appeared in dark skull caps rather than the traditional pointed hat. Their leader, Will Morris, wore a dark evening suit and bow tie. They performed annually at Aberystwyth during the period 1919-1924, following earlier years spent entertaining in Birmingham from 1908.

CASTLE ENTERTAINMENT
UNCLE TOMMY

Tommy Dixon, who originally came from Walsall, successfully recreated the presence of Negro minstrels in Britain, when, with his brother Wally, he formed a troupe in Aberystwyth in 1937. When new forms of music and entertainment come along, the past is inclined to become old fashioned. Minstrelsy nationwide fell into that description with the onset of stage variety, by the concert parties, in music halls, and on radio. The more sedate performances of the minstrels began to appear at a disadvantage. Due to ill health, Tommy's brother returned to the Midlands, leaving Tommy to determine the future. Nonetheless, the decision to stay was taken by Tommy Dixon, which led to a run of summer seasons lasting about ten years, from the spring of 1937, through the period of the Second World War and into the era of post war seaside revival. (Some details from: '*The Illustrated Victorian Song Book*, John Abbott Web site. Also from conversations with the late Dr Ron Walker.)

They were given the opportunity to perform in a small theatre erected below the south castle tower, in an area which had been levelled for its construction. With a space for adequate open air seating, an audience would be enticed to the performances by Tommy hailing a request for their company on a megaphone. If the weather was inclement, performances would be held in the

Uncle Tommy's minstrels in 1939. Photographer: Pickford. Collection: Peter Henley.

nearby Parish Hall. They also performed on the new bandstand and at many local events throughout the summer months. They were known initially as *Uncle Tommy's Minstrels*, then as *Uncle Tommy's Merry Mascots* and, in 1940, as *Uncle Tom Dixon's Pierrots*. Whilst the 'Uncles' wore black and orange, lozenge-shaped Harlequin costumes with large white collars, small white skull caps, and blackened faces with broad white lips, the 'Aunties' wore ballerina style costumes, to show off their legs. They played banjo, ukulele and piano accompanied by an extensive range of percussion instruments. Performances were offered daily, with a changing programme throughout the week. The format of each show was identical: slapstick and comedy sketches followed by solo spots for each performer. By 1940, they were described as the only minstrel troupe in Britain.

The constraints of the Second World War were

lightly felt during the first year, but by the summer of 1940, four of his minstrels had departed for war service. Regardless of the loss, Uncle Tommy continued to provide for the now limited number of visitors with his al fresco sea-side entertainment. They continued as a performing group until the late 1940s.

Mr Emlyn Edwards, formerly of Aberystwyth, remembers the minstrels of Uncle Tommy's and recalled their names and acts:

Uncle Ronnie
A 'vertically challenged', knock-about comedian, specialising in prat falls, who acted as a foil and feed for Uncle Tommy.

Uncle Al
He sang light romantic numbers and performed a sort of soft-shoe shuffle.

Uncle George
He was the pianist and *Basso profundo* and featured songs such as *On the road to Mandalay*, *Old Father Thames* and other late Edwardian ballads.

Uncle Tommy
Tommy Dixon, an interlocutor, comedian and singer of funny songs such as *I do like to be in good company* and *The day we went to Wembley for the cup tie*.

Uncle Wat
He sang George Formby songs.

Uncle Jock
He was a Glaswegian, who sang Harry Lauder numbers, and sang light romantic songs in duet with the only soubrette in the show, Aunty Shirley.

Aunty Shirley
Shirley Twiddy came to Aberystwyth in 1936, to entertain children on the Castle and later joined Tommy Dixon in the Minstrels.

Aunty Doris
The one member of the company who is absent from the photograph is Tommy's formidable wife Doris, who sold the tickets from her little kiosk and generally looked after the finances. She also had her own spot in the shows.

We children loved the Haunted House sketch, with a ghost covered by a white sheet. This gave us the opportunity to shout out, '*IT'S BEHIND YOU!*'

Almost at the end of a show, Uncle Tommy would announce the children's *Go as you please* competition. We would rush onto the stage and lustily bawl out, 'W*e are the Ovaltinies', happy girls and boys,*' before performing our individual piece. The winner by a show of hands would go on to the Friday night *All winners' final*.

To end the show, the full company would link arms with each other and sing a variety of sentimental songs, encouraging the audience to join in, which they did with a will. Many of the artists (as they liked to call themselves) came back year after year. Most of them were recruited from adverts in *Variety* or other

UNCLE TOMMY

My clearest memory of 'Uncle Tommy' is not what you might think-
I see him still, that August afternoon in diamond Pierrot suit and bobble cap,
Striding down North Parade with megaphone in hand,
Announcing in thin distorted voice to all the town the total surrender of the Japanese.

You could see his company on summer afternoons
Performing, diamond gold and black, on the bandstand.
They sang, cracked jokes, danced to accordion and piano
In the great tradition of the British seaside;
I thought them wonderful and swelled with pride
When called up to the stage to join them in an action song.
I looked down at the audience smiling just at me
And as I flapped my elbows and wiggled wrists
I knew my destiny was to hold them spellbound evermore!

Boys and girls - we were the lifeblood of his show -
The wide-eyed Kelly dolls who bounced back every time,
Pleased to be knocked down by such illustrious stars!

In the evenings when the company moved
To that little wooden stage beneath the South Tower of the castle
We would go too and sit through the performance yet again,
Waiting for the 'talent contest' to begin.
Then we would flock on stage and stand in solemn rows
As one by one we would be introduced by Uncle Tommy
To the long-suffering audience steeling itself again
For off-key songs and wooden dances aped from Hollywood and Busby Berkeley!
In vain I waited for a talent scout to whisk me straight away
To Metro Goldwyn Mayer and a life of fame.
I had to be happy with a three penny bit
And lukewarm kudos from those who'd seen it all before.

I've never known who 'Uncle Tommy' was or why
He suddenly stopped coming for the summer season-
Perhaps he died or got too old to cope
With all the energy it takes to get an audience going.

One year, however, there was a new, sophisticated troupe
Performing on the Bandstand in the afternoons –
One with a conjuror named Weston Vivian
Who could make coins appear and disappear behind your ears,.
And a very pretty blue tulle girl who danced and sang
And stayed in OUR house – so I gave THEM all my loyalty instead
And never thought of Uncle Tommy until the years
Had sifted through my childhood and brought him striding
Through my memory with his megaphone!

A delightful 2004 poem about Uncle Tommy, recalling youthful days in the late 1940s, by Mary Mestecky, née Williams, who lived with her parents, the late Jack & Mary Williams, at 68 North Parade, Aberystwyth., and who now lives near Loughborough:

stage magazines. Their winters were spent working in Northern music halls or resting.

They didn't earn a lot, and many who *digged* with us seemed to survive on tinned foods, which they advertised in some of their gags. Their skins suffered, too, because of their daily applications of black grease paint. Judging by today's standards, I suppose it was good, clean, family entertainment, totally free from smut and innuendo, and our parents were quite happy for us to go to Uncle Tommy's. I do not know exactly when it finished. I remember speaking to Tommy outside his house at the bottom of High Street, in the very early 1950s. He was a shadow of his former self, complaining about the way variety was going. As I left him, he smiled and uttered his famous catch phrase, '*Gerrr away*.'

(Recollections of Uncle Tommy and his minstrels by Emlyn Edwards.)

HARPISTS

Many pierrot and minstrel troupes relied upon the harp as an accompanying instrument, along with the flute and violin. The musical dynamic of these selected instruments would be sufficient to support limited outdoor vocal performances in the relative quietness of the castle's isolated venue.

From the late Victorian era, entertainment was allowed to take place within the inner ward of the castle, close to the south tower. The limited space available, in comparison to the large, central, open area within the Gorsedd stones nearby, possibly inhibited continued use here in the 20th century

During the 1930s, the promenade strollers heading for Castle Point from the pier would be entertained by a busking harpist close to the castle's north tower. He would have transported his instrument there on a small, two-wheeled trolley, which he has parked on the road. In front he has positioned his upturned hat on a small stand, to attract a few pennies from appreciative passers by.

Collection: Shirley Evans, Prospect Street, Aberystwyth.
Photographer: Unknown.

Aber Prom

An early 20th century troupe of minstrels performing to a small but intimate audience close to the south tower within the outer ward of Aberystwyth Castle. A variety of acts that would also include comedy and banter would perform at this location. A small canvas enclosure would be erected within the tower, to serve as a changing room.

Collection: Ceredigion Museum. Photographer unknown.

CONCERT PARTIES

TOM JOHNSON

Although it is considered that the golden years of the Concert Party occurred between the wars, from 1919-1939, it is established that, by 1910, this broader, modern style of entertainment had emerged at Aberystwyth. Several members of the departing Gilbert Rogers Company, that had previously appeared locally, had joined the ranks of the evolving company of *Tom Johnson and his Yachtsmen*. They had arrived as the chosen annual summer entertainment, and returned to the town for the next four years, up to the onset of the Great War in 1914. It is possible that the introduction of entertainment in the form of concert parties for servicemen during wartime may have had an influence on the seaside performing style. T W Johnson dressed his troupe in several guises, beginning with the very popular pseudo-naval outfit of white officer's style suits and peaked caps and, then, in a formal, theatrical, military evening dress, worn for his *Military Night*. The next variation, remarkably, was an assembly of Cowboys and Indians in his *Western Company*, complete with a stage back-drop depicting a North American mountain scene and forests. It is likely that this stage set would have been used within the new Pier Pavilion. The *Yachtsmen* finally extended their repertoire in performance in a wooden theatre, similar in size to Catlin's but with patriotic buntings and shields decorating the front. It had been erected about 1910, below the north wall of the Castle, where the putting green is today. The company of nine provided musical and comedy shows, and dressed in *operatic* style costumes.

ELLISON'S ENTERTAINERS

J W Ellison went into partnership with the well known beach entertainer Harry Gold in 1907, to provide beach entertainment in the Thanet area of Kent. Within a few years they had spread their wings, offering with success outdoor shows at Cleethorpes, Withersea, Hastings, Aberystwyth, Ashford and their base at Brighton. They introduced specially constructed, self-contained stages, and made early use of electricity as outdoor illumination. At that time, Gold and Ellison were granted a patent for improvements in portable al-fresco stages, which they put to good use to enhance their performances. (Terry Wheeler, Ramsgate Civic Society on Harry Gold)

They constantly altered the name of their troupe in an attempt to create increased appeal. One title used following the Great War, from 1919, was *The Yachtsmen Concert Party,* described by them as, '*Now better than its pre-war standard.*' Previously, in 1917, Ellison had introduced an All Lady Concert Party of eight to the entertainment scene at Brighton.

Ellison brought a concert party group of eight or nine to Aberystwyth for several seasons, from June 1914 and throughout the Great War, until the

In this 1910 photograph taken opposite St David's wharf in Aberystwyth Harbour, Tom W Johnson and seven of his *Yachtsmen* in nautical gear are seen aboard a Morecambe Bay prawner with its skipper and mate.

Photographer: Pickford.
Collection: Peter Davis

A 1912 Pickford Studio photograph of Tom Johnson with his ten *Yachtsmen* and *Yachtswomen* in their performing nautical attire.

Collection: Peter Henley

mid 1920s, performing within the castle grounds and other venues. Each day, they erected canvas awnings around a small dais in the centre of the castle grounds, and not only provided seating for the audience, but also a covered awning to protect them during wet weather. The men wore formal outfits of dark or chequered suits, white shirts and black bow ties, whilst the ladies appeared in full-length, white cotton dresses. In later seasons, the men had added straw hats and spats to their attire, while the ladies wore wide-brimmed, fashionable bonnets. They would have performed three times daily at various locations, and, no doubt, a special arrangement would have been made to transport their piano on a trolley to each pitch for their resident pianist, Billy Draper. The troupe stayed in lodgings locally throughout the summers and two members of Ellison's party, in particular, are remembered by Evan Andrews of South Road: Uncle Charlie and Aunty Witty. They had stayed with his parents in Prospect Street during the 1916-1923 period. Ellison's partner, Harry Gold, accompanied him in Aberystwyth for several seasons, serving as co-performer and business manager, basing himself, between performances, in a booking office with telephone (number Aberystwyth 10) within the castle grounds. (Advertisement in the *Cambrian News,* (3. 7. 1914))

In an advert in July 1914, J W Ellison, as the leader of *Ellison's Entertainers*, a previously unheard of group in the town, keenly emphasised that no vulgarity is permitted at any of his entertainments and that each and every artist is an experienced performer. Following their debut, they had provided a new awning, to protect their patrons from excessive heat, and reiterated that in no way would it interfere with the view from outside the barriers. (*Cambrian News,* 3. 7. 1914. NLW)

CASTLE GROUNDS

J.W.ELLISON'S ENTERTAINERS

At 11, 3 and 7.30 daily Wet or Fine

Pay one visit and you will come again and again

No vulgarity is permitted at any of Mr Ellison's entertainments

----

EACH ANY EVERY ARTIST IS AN EXPERIENCED PERFORMER

The new awning is now complete to seat Patrons from rain or excessive heat whilst in no way interfering with the view from outside the barriers.

SPECIAL COSTUME NIGHTS!   SPECIAL COSTUME NIGHTS!

MONDAY (Bank holiday) - PIERROT NIGHT

WEDNESDAY - SCOTCH NIGHT

FRIDAY EVENING - DRESS REQUEST NIGHT

Seats at popular prices may be booked for any performance without extra charge at the
CASTLE GROUNDS
Business Manager: Harry Gold   Telephone: Aberystwyth 10

Music History

The visiting performers were obviously keen to provide a particular standard of entertainment, which was equally expected by the tourists and controlling authorities. Understandably, the character and permitted level of entertainment suited what could easily be described as correct for a town the size of Aberystwyth, that was shaped not only by the people that lived there but also by the people that visited.

It was not easy to please all visitors, who compared the facilities and developments discovered locally with those, perhaps, of more familiar, larger towns elsewhere. An observation by the local press, under their 1914 'Summer Season' column reported that, '*Visitors find themselves unexpectedly in what may be called back-streets and are unreasonably surprised that the exclusiveness of fashionable squares in large towns is not provided by small seaside resorts.*' (*Cambrian News,* 17.7. 1914. NLW)

'THE YACHTSMEN' CONCERT PARTY

Proprietors: MESSRS. GOLD & ELLISON.

Also at MARGATE, BRIGHTON, ABERYSTWYTH, etc.

DAILY at 11.0, 3.0 and 7.0.

Special Engagement of New Artistes and Old Favourites.

THIS CONCERT PARTY IS NOW BETTER THAN ITS PRE-WAR STANDARD.

EVERY EVENING.

VALUABLE PRIZES will be presented by MR. "TIT BITS" to patrons who are holders of a current issue of "Tit Bits" or "Woman's Life." Secure a copy of either of these two publications, and take a sporting chance of gaining one of these Handsome Presents.

Thursday Afternoon—LOVE LETTER WRITING for GENTS.
Friday Afternoon—BOYS' BOOT LACING COMPETITION.

Competitions Every Afternoon.   Prizes by "Tit Bits."

SPECIAL COSTUME CONCERTS—Tuesday and Thursday Evenings

SEATS - - 3d., 5d. & 9d.

A small poster advertising the *Yachtsmen* shows given by the concert parties of Harry Gold and Ellison at Margate, Brighton and Aberystwyth during the 1920s. Audience participation comedy items included *Love letter writing for Gents* and *Boy's boot-lacing competition*. The show prizes were sponsored by the popular magazine, *Tit-bits*.

Collection: British Music Hall Society

Aber Prom

Ellison's entertainers photographed in the studio of Gyde & Pickford, in Pier Street, Aberystwyth, c. 1922. The popularity of formal 'concert party' attire by seasoned imported players is apparent. The 1920s also provided much new song material to challenge the popular victorian and edwardian tunes.

Photographer: Gyde & Pickford.
Collection: Peter Henley

During the 1923 summer show season, Ellison's eight entertainers appeared on the castle grounds in an alternative style of concert party outfits. Their dress included nautical-type, peaked caps and dark, double-breasted jackets, with starched, pointed, shirt-collars and bow ties for the men, while the females wore knotted headscarves and light summer dresses. The photograph was produced for them by Pickfords of Pier Street, for sale that year as postcards. Pickfords cleverly devised a technique of creating a montage of eight vignette studio portraits of the entertainers. J W Ellison appears, in costume, second from the top left.

HARRY GOLD

Harry Gold was born Patrick Henry James Ricks, on the Isle of Jersey in 1866, and began his career as a busker on the streets of London. Soon after, he moved to America, where he changed his name and joined the vaudeville scene there for several years. He returned to Ramsgate, where he formed his own troupe of pierrots, on the sands at nearby Margate, in 1903. He partnered with J W Ellison to form *Gold's Smart Serenaders*, eventually creating *Gold and Ellison's Yachtsmen* in 1907. They were a huge success and employed further troupes to play at Ramsgate, Brighton and Aberystwyth. Harry Gold's Irish parents, living on Jersey in the late Victorian period, had encouraged him to develop a fine Irish style voice, which he used at great length during his career. At the height of the concert party era, Gold would travel to each outpost of his troupes in turn and join in with them during the summer periods, often bringing with him members recruited back home in Ramsgate. In 1914, when Ellison formed his own concert parties in Brighton and Aberystwyth, Gold joined the troupe here as business manager and soloist.

A decade later, in his 65th year, he formed the *Harry Gold's Aberystwyth Entertainer*s and brought his concert party to the resort in 1931, to perform for the summer visitors. His group of eight included two female singers, with the men dressed in blazers and white-topped peaked caps, and the ladies in fashionable 1930s leisure wear outfits and caps. In 1939, when World War Two intervened, Gold withdrew from the entertainment business. He never returned to perform in the post conflict era, and died in 1946. (Extracts - Terry Wheeler, Ramsgate Civic Society – 'Harry Gold-Ramsgate entertainer extraordinary')

Harry Gold's Aberystwyth Entertainers, 1931
Collection: Ron Cowell. Photographer unknown

The entertainer Harry Gold (1866-1946) photographed in the studio of Gyde and Pickford, in Pier Street, Aberystwyth, in 1916.

Collection: Peter Henley

Music History

HARRY GOLD'S
Aberystwyth Entertainers
July -- August -- September.

Return of the Aberystwyth Favourites
A REAL CONCERT PARTY
Entertainment and Fresh Air Combined

MARINA TERRACE BANDSTAND
Concerts daily at 11-0 & 3-0

CASTLE GROUNDS PAVILION
Concerts every evening at 7-30

::: POPULAR PRICES :::

Manager... ...(for Harry Gold)... ...Reg Irving

A poster advertising Harry Gold's Aberystwyth Entertainers used in the 1932 Aberystwyth Guide and Souvenir.
Collection: Peter Henley

PROMENADE ORCHESTRAS

In the mid 19th century, most hired musical ensembles comprised mainly brass and reed players, although the introduction of strings into their formation is evident in that period, creating in reality a light orchestra that played both in the Pier Pavilion and in the early circular bandstands. The brief description of all of the above musical groups, especially in the local press and in concert programmes and posters, was often simply *The band*.

The word band, today, suggests a musical assembly that does not include stringed instruments. The word band, at the turn of the 20th century, could have been a general description of an instrumental group that would have been predominantly brass but could have included woodwind and string players. Nevertheless, small orchestras did play on the promenade, from the Victorian era. The University College Music Department would have maintained its distinctly classical role, existing within a short distance of the music performed around the corner on the promenade, although the difference in presentation and style would have been enormous.

The promenade band-cum-orchestra would not necessarily have adhered to the available, original, classical composers' scoring. Music for brass bands during the late 19th century was being written in a form that made it easier for amateur players to read and play. As a consequence, wind instruments were generally available from the instrument manufacturers only in high pitch, for use in brass bands, until the 1950s, to suit this easier form of arrangement. The brass band publishers, therefore, were isolated from the concert pitch music of orchestral playing and, consequently, transposed desirable, popular, orchestral melodies to suit the modified pitch of the band instruments. For those players venturing outside the high pitch world, it meant an adjustment (if at all possible) to low pitch, and a possibly discordant entry into the new world of concert pitch. The Professor of Music at Aberystwyth in the 1920s, Walford Davies, persuaded Jack Edwards, the conductor of the town band, to help him with the introduction of wind playing into the College Orchestra. Whenever a particular player was having difficulty tuning to the orchestra at the recommended pitch of C (C552), he would suggest that, if they persisted without solving the problem, then all the milk in Aberystwyth would turn sour! (Extract from '*The Spiritual Pilgrims*' by Ian Parrott, 1964)

The local militia band continued to maintain a total wind band formation; although there is evidence that an orchestra in military dress was hired to play for the entire 1928 season, under the directorship of Stephen Evans, who, for many years during the 1930s, was the Aberystwyth Town Bandmaster.

Concerts in true orchestral style were performed on the pier and bandstand by the established Aberystwyth Municipal Orchestra at the turn of the 20th century. While their conductor, Philip Lewis, shared his duties with the London Symphony Orchestra, he continued to play with the local

Before the permanent Jubilee bandstand was built in 1935, variations on a cast iron, Victorian pagoda-style survived until that period. A small 1920s orchestra is playing, in this enclosed version on the promenade, to an audience that has paid three pence each to sit and listen to the music. The number card attached to the central pillar indicated the piece of music being played, which the audience could have found in their programmes.

Collection: Peter Parry. Photographer unknown

Aber Prom

Evered Davies continued in the role of Musical Director of the Aberystwyth Municipal Orchestra throughout World War II. He relied heavily upon local musicians to form this 13-piece light Orchestra, including Esme Silver as violinist, Stuart Knussen on cello, Bill Davies the trombonist, Ned Lewis as drummer and young Ronnie Hughes the trumpeter. By 1947, Evered Davies had enlarged the string section and increased the number of players to twenty.

Photographer: Evered Davies. Collection: Peter Henley

Music History

Victor Fleming (1901-1991), who ranked amongst the top orchestral and choral conductors in the UK, played a prominent part in Aberystwyth's music-making during the 1930s. He began playing locally in 1918, at the age of 17, in the town's orchestra, and returned to live and teach in Aberystwyth, becoming the conductor of the Aberystwyth Municipal Orchestra from 1936-38. During this period, he contributed not only to the provision of classical music on the minute, pre-war, circular bandstand, but also in the musical concerts within the town. He is also credited with the honour of assisting in the formation of the Welsh National Opera Company, which he conducted from 1944-1949. He continued his work in music for many years, at Ventnor, in the Isle of Wight, until his death in 1991.

Collection: Mrs Fay Brown, Ventnor Town Library, Isle of Wight.

orchestra, possibly during the Edwardian summers, with imported players. Their orchestra line-up did not exceed eleven players, and would be considered a chamber orchestra today.

The Entertainments and General Purposes Committee of the Town Council was responsible for providing both a summer band and an orchestra every year, from the early 1900s until the 1950s. Initially, this arrangement was made in conjunction with the Aberystwyth Improvement Company, who owned the pier. In 1911, the post of Musical Director was created, to oversee the provision of promenade music for the entire season. The position survived until the last war, when Evered Davies accepted the post for the duration. Later, from the 1950s, the establishment of a Town Council Entertainment Office incorporated the role into its duties.

Between the wars, it would be common practice for the Musical Director to hire professional players, to create a playing formation locally. Local brass players would brush shoulders with imported orchestral musicians in the Promenade Orchestra, which continued to offer light entertainment continuously until the mid 1950s. Daily performances were provided principally in the 1935-built Jubilee bandstand, which could accommodate orchestras of about twenty players, including a pianist. Many well known classical musicians were involved with the Promenade Orchestra, including Gus Cheetham, Victor Fleming, Leslie Ernest, Stuart Knussen and brothers Hayden and Logan Lewis.

'THE BANDSTAND'

Developing Welsh resorts eventually established a style that became synonymous with English towns that were becoming popular with Victorian seekers of park and promenade music. One essential item that became linked with these coastal and inland resorts was the bandstand. Although we regard it as a symbol of Gothic Victorian architecture, its origins can be traced back to the late 18th century, when ornate pleasure domes were erected to house orchestras. One of the earliest examples was built in London's Vauxhall Gardens, while the first one particularly for bands was built in the 1840s, in Cremorne Gardens, also in London. The earliest designs of the emerging bandstands were in fact greatly influenced by oriental architecture.

Following the building of the famous Chinese pagoda in Kew Gardens in 1762, the pagoda bandstand becomes a traditional building in British parks and gardens. Once parks and, of course, promenades, became established, they became associated with the provision of live entertainment. Bands, in particular, were well suited to playing outdoors and, consequently, found themselves instantly popular and were employed with full programmes. As a result, their summer season had been established. Consequently, ironmakers, now in demand for these new cast iron structures, began including them in their catalogues as standardised ready-made kits.

(Extracts from *'Village and Town Bands'*, by Christopher Weir, Shire pub. Ltd. 1981)

Many resorts in the UK were employing these substantial, gothic-style, ornate bandstands to accommodate the players, who, unlike the strolling pierrots and minstrels, required a seating arrangement with music stands and a preferred level of protection from the weather. Modest arrangements were made initially using temporary wooden constructions on the beach. Later in the 19th century, they appeared as circular, turreted, cast iron buildings, with side wings, to encourage the public to sit on the promenade and enjoy the performances. Several variations were brought in from the late 1800s until the early 1930s.

In 1894, in Aberystwyth, the local Bandmaster, Jack Edwards, complained that the temporary bandstand on the beach was unsatisfactory and in poor repair. An alternative wooden structure appeared on the promenade alongside the stone lifeboat launching ramp, and stood for a few seasons, but by 1899, following much debate, the Town Council decided to buy a proper building, based on an established nationwide design, and place it alongside the perimeter wall of the promenade. It was ordered from Macfarlane & Company at a cost of £150 and duly put into use by the Town Band. Several variations on this circular design, with its distinctive pagoda, cone-shaped roof and ornate cast iron pillars, emerged over the following thirty-five years. Side wings were added and seating provided for hire on the promenade. One innovative feature that developed in the early 20th century included the ability to move the stand away from the edge of the sea wall, allowing the listeners to sit around it on the beach. The pitches employed in that period varied from the seaward end of Terrace Road to opposite today's Marine Hotel.

The bandstands had all been quite modest in size and would not have accommodated more than fifteen seated players comfortably. By 1935, following many complaints and the corrosive effects of years of salt and exposure on the iron structures, the decision to build a permanent, Art Deco style, concrete bandstand was made. It was unveiled less than a year after the opening of the revolutionarily designed King's Hall in 1934, to celebrate the Jubilee of George V.

The actual bandstand was similar in size to the earlier shapes, but built in concrete within an outer-walled, open auditorium, with columned electric lights fitted into the outer wall. This central bandstand design was short-lived, probably due to its limiting size and, also, being glazed all round would have made it unbearably hot inside. A modified covered stage was soon built against the seaward inner end of the outer retaining wall. It offered full protection from the weather and could accommodate a light orchestra or brass band in comfort. The audience could sit within the outer wall, on deck chairs, to sunbathe whilst they were being entertained. The bandstand survives today but has been modified to allow listeners to sit under cover.

Associated with performances on the bandstands and the surrounding promenade area over the years has been the provision of folding chairs, commonly described as deckchairs, for the audiences. The very

One of the earliest temporary Victorian bandstands, photographed in 1894. It is, unusually, not the traditional circular shape, although of similar size to the later Gothic style structure. It appears to be built mainly of wood, and does have quite a smart appearance at its location next to the old stone lifeboat launching ramp. There is no apparent seating provided, and it suggests that it may have offered a rather contained form of entertainment to passing promenaders. Alongside it are beach traders selling fruit and seafood.

Collection: National Library of Wales. Photographer: Arthur Lewis

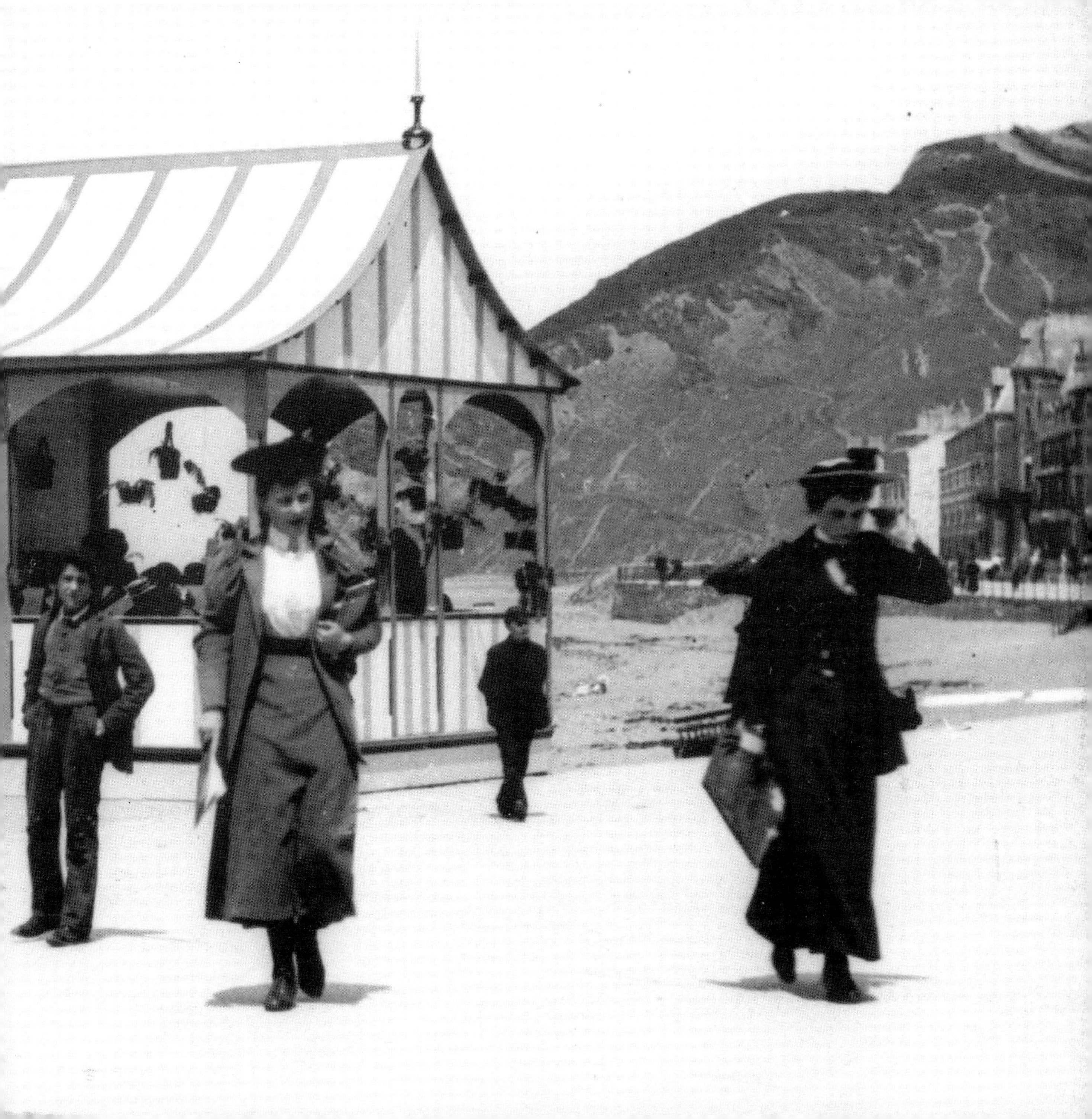

A family group on Aberystwyth beach, c. 1900, pose for the camera with the new bandstand behind them. It was erected in 1899, to accommodate a variety of summertime entertainments, including pierrots, minstrels, brass bands and orchestras. Performances would take place three times daily throughout the season. There appears to be some form of slapstick comedy taking place, while the Gilbert Rogers Minstrels in their white suits wait amongst the large audience for their turn to perform. This style of bandstand was to survive in this location for the next 35 years.

Collection: Ceredigion Museum. Photographer unknown

In 1901 permission had been granted by the town council for an extra entertainment booth and dais to be erected on the beach a short distance northwards of the new permanent, circular, cast iron bandstand. The booth was in reality a square, attractively built, striped hut, with a small flat wooden stage in front, placed near the promenade perimeter wall, directly opposite today's Richmond Hotel.

In the candidly taken photograph are seen Gilbert Rogers' black-faced, performing minstrels entertaining a seated audience. The side wings were probably designed to reduce the interference by sea breezes and also to encourage people off the beach and into the arranged seats, to view the performances. Many strollers would also line the promenade above, to watch the frivolities.

Collection: Ceredigion Museum. Photographer unknown

Aber Prom

popular wood and canvas beach chair emerged in Europe in about 1850 and could be hired for the beach or promenade locally. It survived until the 1980s, never to re-emerge in a modified way. Its development began in Egypt, where it served as a folding chair for commanding officers in the army, during the period 2000-1500 B.C. It continued its popularity, in many forms, particularly for military use, and then it was put to more pleasurable use in modern times, in its classic hammock style, known as a *chaise transatlantique*.

In 1935, this fine example of an Art Deco style, concrete bandstand, within a perimeter wall, was built to replace a succession of short-lived, cast iron structures. The tall, central, cylindrical structure, based on a circular Victorian shape, must have been unsuitable and was removed during the Second World War, to be replaced with an off–centre covered stage within the seaward end of the wall. It was then capable of holding larger orchestras, bands and choirs.

Collection: Peter Henley. Photographer unknown

Music History

The Jubilee Bandstand in the 1950s, within the remodelled inner area. The covered stage has been rebuilt at the seaward end, within the surviving original wall and lamp posts. A band is playing off-stage in the open air deckchair area, in front of a large audience.

Collection: Peter Henley. Photographer unknown

The bandstand interior in July 1985, showing the added, covered auditorium and stage lighting. The photograph was taken during a concert given by the Midleton Band from County Cork, in Eire, conducted by Bandmaster John Curtin.

Collection: Peter Henley

ABERYSTWYTH PIER

Following an increase in inshore passenger-carrying, many British coastal resorts began to build landing stages and jetties as a safe means of transferring fare-paying passengers to and from steamships. These seaward constructions took on a new role, when seaside visitors began using them as a continuation of their promenading. It was not long before enterprising Victorian owners began to offer typical seaside entertainment in purpose-built pavilions along the pier's length. The pier constructed at Aberystwyth was built principally to perpetuate this development of entertainment. Due to the limiting depth of seawater and the adjacency of the College rocks, the pier end as a landing stage never was suitable for large vessels that required sufficient clearance to operate safely. Its pier-end landing stage was limited, therefore, to local craft that offered either short trips along the coast, or a ferry service to outlying, visiting warships etc. The pier that exists today is the second structure on this site; an original, simpler jetty had been built in 1806 but was destroyed in a storm in about 1810.

The present pier was built by the Aberystwyth Promenade Company Limited, under supervision of their engineer, Eugenius Birch. Birch (1818- 1884) was the architect who designed the pier's 800 foot (242 metre) length, and was responsible for designing fourteen British piers He alone is credited for bringing immense joy and happiness into the lives of millions of people, with his pier and aquarium constructions in Britain. Aberystwyth Pier was partly opened as the first Welsh pleasure pier, with great celebration, on Good Friday 1865, shortly after the coming of the railway to the town. As a result, 5,000 people travelled by train to the town for the opening. A total of 7,000 paid one penny each to walk the length of the pier that day. The pier had a bandstand at the seaward end, which, unfortunately, was swept away in an 1866 storm, only two years after the opening. The end was refurbished in 1872, and a new bandstand was built on it.

Further rebuilding took place during the following decades and, by 1896, the pier had gained a large landward pavilion and a seaward end theatre. The pavilion itself, which could seat an audience of 2,000, would provide a constant flow of live entertainment throughout the year, for the next thirty years. The pier was formally opened by Her Royal Highness Princess Alexandra, accompanied by Prince Edward, in 1896, and became known ever since as the Royal Pier Pavilion. The pleasure pier, without doubt, was an immense attraction nationwide, offering the thrill of strolling its length, jostling amongst the other trippers, the enticement of the coin slot machines, the clairvoyant and phrenologist in their dimly lit rooms, the band and minstrels at the far end of the elongation above the waves, the sea air and sunshine, with lots of fun and laughter. It all combined to make the day out a memorable experience. Such was its success, combined with the ingenuity of the Victorians that no fewer than seventy-eight piers were built between 1860 and 1910.

At larger British resorts, the stars of the London

Music History

Prior to its expansion that would include a large pavilion in 1896, the pier survived as a simple construction for thirty years. Its elevations boasted a pier-end theatre and walkway. This early 1890s photograph advertises the performances of the town band, Sunday sacred concerts and Harry Collins' minstrels.

Collection: Ceredigion Library

Aber Prom

The railings and kiosks of the Aberystwyth Royal Pier Pavilion display a galaxy of posters, including Cambrian Railways trips to London, a recital by a pianist, recorded music provided by a gramophone, the services of a phrenologist, performances of strolling players, and a small sign, saying, 'Admission 2d' (two pence). There are also several assorted coin slot machines in front of the magnificent, late Victorian, gothic pavilion facade. Above the central door was a plaque commemorating the opening of the pavilion by Her Royal Highness, The Princess of Wales, in 1896.

Photographer: Emile Thomas Evans. Date: c. 1903. Collection: Peter Henley

This late Victorian interior of the Royal Pier Pavilion at Aberystwyth shows the large auditorium and stage. An enormous variety of performances took place here, before it was altered in the 1940s to accommodate tiered seating for the modern cinema. Many famous stage celebrities performed here during the initial thirty years of the 20th century. The pier provided a stage for political speeches, wartime concerts, variety acts and sacred music concerts.

Date: c.1900. Photographer: Unknown. Collection: Ceredigion Museum

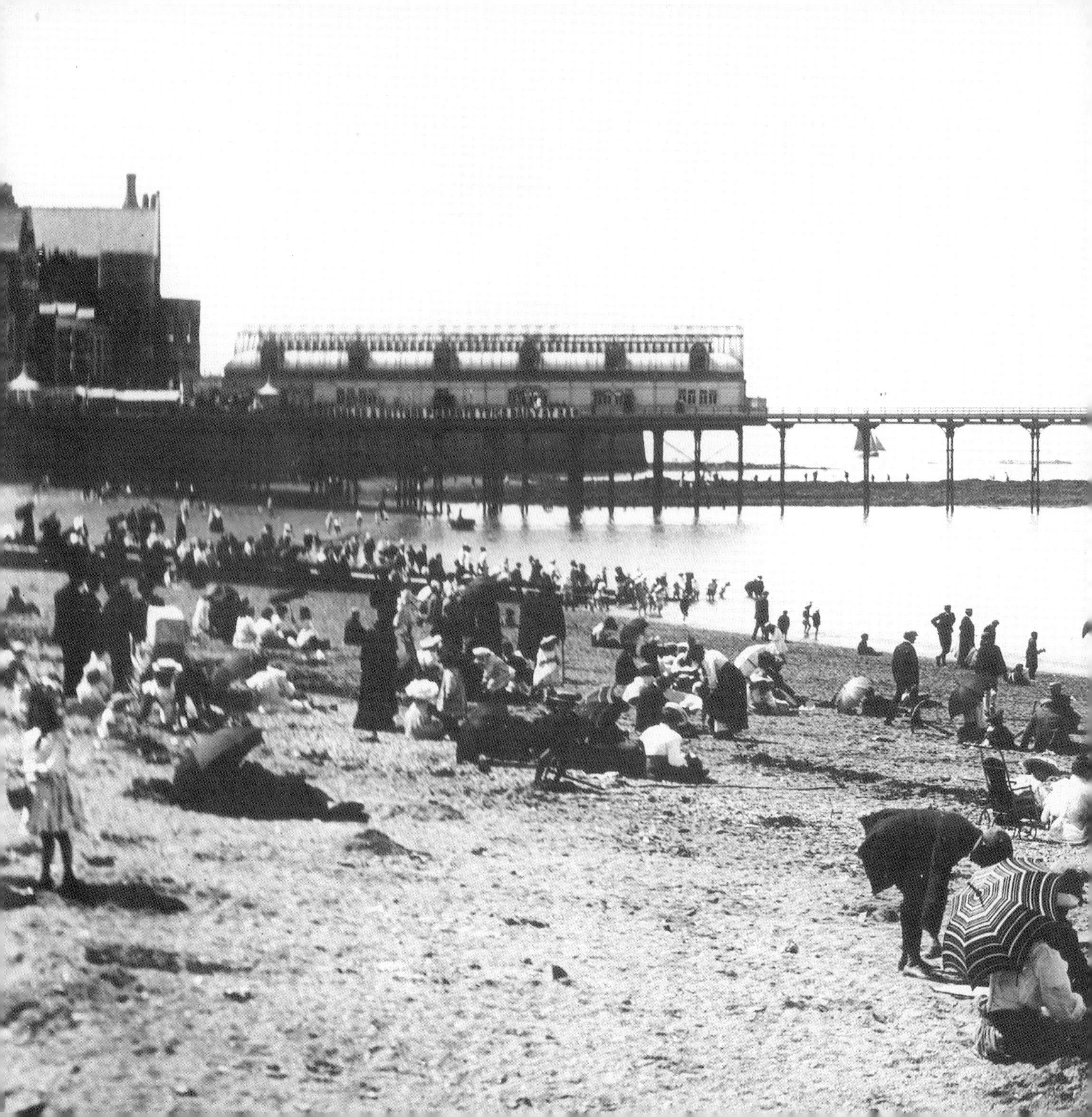

A 1907 Edwardian, busy summer beach scene at Aberystwyth, showing the full 800 foot length of the pier with its pavilion, end theatre, bandstand and landing stage. A long board along the railings advertises: 'Adeler and Sutton Pierrots twice daily.' At the water's edge is the pleasure boat *Lizzie*, plying for trade, with a Morecambe Bay Nobby fishing boat drying its sails, and a beach placard offering trips on the steam boat *May*.

Photographer: Emile Thomas Evans, Aberystwyth. Collection: Peter Henley

Aber Prom

Music Hall were lured by the success of the seaside pier theatres, during the Victorian summers. Several made brief appearances on Aber pier, including the famous actor George Robey. The pier came to be regarded as one of the premier places of entertainment in west Wales; later offering dancing in its ballroom and live music daily in its fashionable café. Films replaced the declining interest in live summer shows in 1922, and in a 1923 advert it was described as a super-cinema, offering twice daily shows. As an alternative, live music could be listened to at the pier-head bandstand. The late Les Dawson humorously described summer shows as, 'Music Hall with salt.' Storms in January 1938 took away most of the seaward elevations, truncating its length by half, to 300 feet (91m); the lost portion has never been replaced.

The modern cinema closed following serious fires there in 1955, and in the bar and foyer on January 3rd, 1961. The large, sloping-floored auditorium was transformed into a bingo hall in July 1965. During the 1970s, the entire landward pavilion frontage was boarded up for a decade. Thankfully, the new owners sympathetically exposed and restored the magnificent gothic style, Victorian facade to its former glory in the 1980s. The pavilion was divided in height, when a new floor was inserted in the 1990s, obliterating the imposing Victorian pavilion's iron pillars and arched roof structure in the process.

This advert from 1931 shows the Pier Pavilion ballroom and upstairs cafeteria that survived in this form until the 1960s. It later became a gaming and pin ball room before conversion into a billiard hall. The advert described it as *famed for dainty teas*. Collection: Peter Henley

Music History

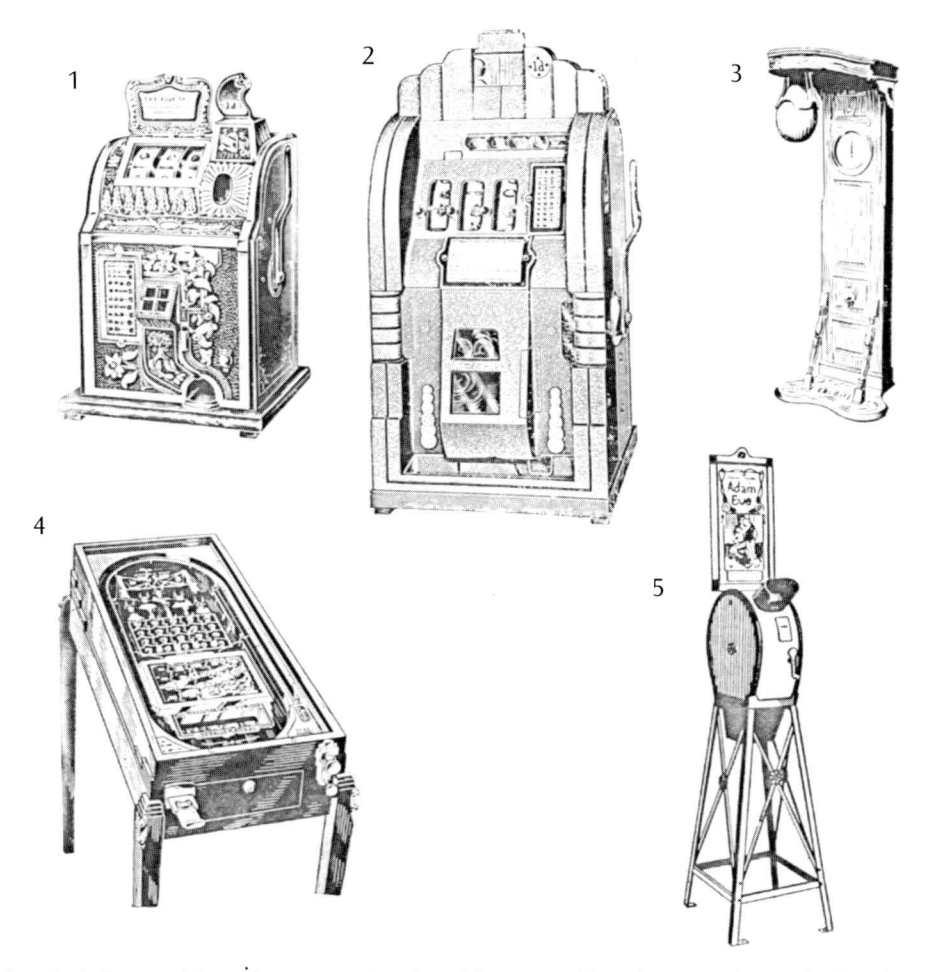

A selection of typical slot machines, from a 1930s advertising pamphlet, that were in use in the Pier amusement arcade and in 'Tuson's' basement of the King's Hall from the period 1930-1950s.

1. Early mechanical gambling fruit machine
2. A version of gaming machine.
3. A boxing punch ball strength indicator.
4. An electrically operated bagatelle.
5. A 'What the Butler Saw' illuminated 'peep-show'.

These were all pre-decimalisation machines that operated for one penny. They did not survive into the decimal coinage era, introduced on February 15th, 1971.

Collection: Peter Henley

KING'S HALL

The decision to build a new, multi-purpose hall in the town was made in the early 1930s. The chosen site, where the 120-bedroom Waterloo Hydro Hotel had previously stood, at the centre of the Marine Terrace, on the promenade was ideal. The site had lain derelict for 15 years, following a disastrous fire in 1919, which totally gutted the hotel. In 1934, the new Municipal Hall and Palm Court was opened with great celebration. It took over several duties of the Coliseum Theatre in Terrace Road, which had previously been multi-purpose and greatly used for the University's shows and for examinations. The King's Hall's large stage, wide auditorium and spacious balcony guaranteed its use for a variety of concerts, dances and summer shows. It had an upstairs cafeteria and roof garden and in its basement was an amusement arcade. Its windowed, concrete facade incorporated a tower, clock and flagpole.

A year after its opening, to celebrate the Jubilee of King George V and his visit to the town, it was renamed the King's Hall. Its imposing Art Deco architecture was in contrast to the 19th century terraced houses and hotels along the promenade, and did invite criticism.

The government had decreed that all theatres and cinemas should close at the declaration of war, on September 3rd, 1939, but the Chief Constable of Cardiganshire decided that he had discretionary powers to permit performances locally, provided that air raid precautions were taken.

Somewhat to the surprise of the Charles Simon's Repertory Company, the show had to go on. On Monday, September 4th, 1939, the King's Hall was said to have been the only theatre in the United Kingdom to be open for business. (Extracted from 'Wireless Whispers', written by 'Peter' in the *Cambrian News,* September 1959)

The location and size of the King's Hall auditorium and stage were of great benefit to the university, as part of the close town and gown relationship. The university's reliance upon it declined as the student facilities developed on Penglais. Coupled with the detection of structural problems and diminishing use, it was demolished in 1989. The site is now occupied by the Neuadd y Brenin apartments and shops and an open seating area. During its 55-year lifetime it had been regarded as the hub of entertainment locally and is sadly missed. Many famous people appeared there, including *The Rolling Stones*, and prime ministers Harold Wilson and James Callaghan. Many famous orchestras performed there, including the London Symphony, conducted by the famous Pierre Monteux, and performances were given by cellist Paul Tortellier. The promenade's association with indoor entertainment was overwhelmingly curtailed until, shortly before the destruction of the hall, the new and vibrant Arts Centre opened on Penglais in the 1970s, guaranteeing the continuation of entertainment in the town.

Music History

A 1937 advert for the King's Hall, showing the modern Art Deco facade, interior seating and stage. The auditorium was easily transformed into a dance hall.

Collection: Ceredigion Museum

During the mid 1930s, the Follies Dance Band of Aberystwyth augmented the interest in ballroom dancing locally with their seven-piece formation. They're seen in September 1934, in front of the original stage back-drop scenery, in the recently opened Municipal Hall, later to be called the King's Hall. The players include Laurie Morris, Eddie Beddoes, Cecil Hutchings, Percy Moore and Percy Thomas.

Photographer: Glyn Pickford.
Collection: Peter Henley

The King's Hall Dance Band. During the 1950s, the ever popular King's Hall on Marine Terrace continued to host Saturday night dances, with a resident band led by Jim Hayes (far left) on saxophone. They continued to provide Latin-American numbers along with the popular strict tempo waltzes and fox-trots. In the foreground is the singer Pegi Edwards, who delighted the gyrating dancers with her deep, crooning voice. Pegi could often be heard on Welsh radio and television during the early days of ITV transmissions. Many of the musicians were local workers, who kept the dance band going in their spare time. Collection: Peter Henley. Photographer unknown

Music History

THE JIMMY LEACH BAND

During the 1950s, the Borough Council's entertainment committee employed a resident, professional, summer season dance band called *Jimmy Leach and his Organolians*. They were hired to play on the promenade bandstand during the day and in the King's Hall in the evening, for local dances and concerts. They became very popular with locals and visitors and returned to the town for many seasons until the 1960s.

Jimmy Leach (1905-1975) played regularly for the Northern Dance Orchestra as both pianist and organist. He frequently broadcast with his own band on the BBC Radio Light Programme and, in particular, the popular lunchtime live programme *Workers Playtime*. Amongst Jimmy Leach's many popular arrangements for his band were *Ebony Silver* and *Serenade to a lonely Star*.

Jimmy Leach is seated at the King's Hall organ with his band of *Organolians*. Collection: Ceredigion Museum. Photographer unknown

Aber Prom

Peggy Royston, August 3rd, 1975.

Peggy Royston came from London, with her family, to live in Aberystwyth, in the 1930s. She and her brother performed as entertainers and acrobatic dancers on the Coliseum stage before its days as a cinema. With her husband, Ernie Morgan, as Musical Director, they organised dancing shows and pantomime charity events with great success for many years in the King's Hall, until the 1980s. Their very first charity concert was for the Lynmouth flood disaster victims in 1952. It became the first of countless charity events produced by them. Their efforts are dearly remembered but sadly unheralded. Peggy died in 2006, aged 93.

Collection & Photographer: Peter Henley

The Peggy Royston Dancers. In January 1972, the *Peggy Royston Tiny Tots* and *Go-Go Dancers* took part in a charity Musical Revue in the King's Hall. They were captured earlier, on 30th November 1971, in this photograph taken during rehearsals for the show. They are left to right: Sandy Stein; Beverley Milner; Beverley Gemmel; Hazel Jones; Alison Jones; Linda Stein; Ann Kerslake and Marita Pugh.

Peggy Royston had little difficulty in finding willing locals to take part in her wonderful pantomimes in the King's Hall. Performers, young and old, stage hands, costume makers, scenery artists, prop carpenters and publicity volunteers would offer their time as Peggy herself trained the dancers and performed with them. Each season the proceeds from their efforts would go towards a deserving local charity.

Collection & Photography: Peter Henley

Aber Prom

On March 15th, 1970, BBC Cymru recorded their Welsh television pop show, *Disc a Dawn*, in the King's Hall. Taking part in the programme was the Trawsfynydd-based group, *Y Pelydrau*. The show was produced by Rhydderch Jones, with the Welsh celebrity Ronnie Williams as compere. Local children were invited to participate in the dancing.

Collection & Photography: Peter Henley.
Acknowledgements: Mr Wil Owen and Miss Elin Wyn Davies, BBC Wales Cardiff.

Music History

The trio, *Yr Aur Leisiau*.

During the summers of the 1970s the King's Hall was popular for its Old Tyme Music Hall shows, in which local talent had the opportunity to perform. The *Aur Leisiau, a* trio of girls from Llanfarian & district, delighted the audiences during the 1975 season with their renderings of Welsh songs. They were trained by Miss Megan Jones of Abermagwr, and we see Enfys Jones, Carys Wyn Jones and Janice Evans relaxing between rehearsals on August 3rd, 1975.

Acknowledgement: Tom Parry Edwards & Mrs Meinir Holliday. Photograph: Peter Henley

Aber Prom

CRYSTAL VAUDEVILLE COMPANY

During the years 1972-75, a group of locals decided to put on charity summer shows in the King's Hall, based on the BBC's Olde Tyme Music Hall format, popular in Victorian times. Based on the name of the Crystal Palace public house in Queen's Road, popular with musicians, the Crystal Vaudeville Company was born.

The Director and instigator of the shows was Leonard 'Bill' James, a lecturer in the University's Music Department and Bandmaster of the Aberystwyth Silver Band. Many acts were created, including a traditional style jazz band, formed from within the show group. Its Musical Director was Dr David Russell Hulme.

The members of Mrs Ferguson's Chorus, in period costumes, join the Master of Ceremonies, Andy Thompson, for a stroll along the promenade during a break in performances of the Crystal Vaudeville Olde Tyme Music hall shows in the King's Hall in August 1973. Collection and photography: Peter Henley

Crystal Vaudeville Temperance Foot Warmers Band, August 3rd, 1975, King's Hall, Aberystwyth

Left to right: Chris Tremlett, Drums, Geography postgraduate; Fred Potter, Piano, Science Computer Analyst; Ivor Pemberthy, Tuba, HGV Driver; David Russell Hulme, Conductor/Drums, Music postgraduate; John R. Davies, Trumpet, Jeweller; Colin Rudeforth, Clarinet, Agricultural Scientist; John P. Evans, Solo Trombone, Hospital Radiographer; Peter Henley, Trombone, University Technician; Mike Taylor, Banjo, School Teacher

Aber Prom

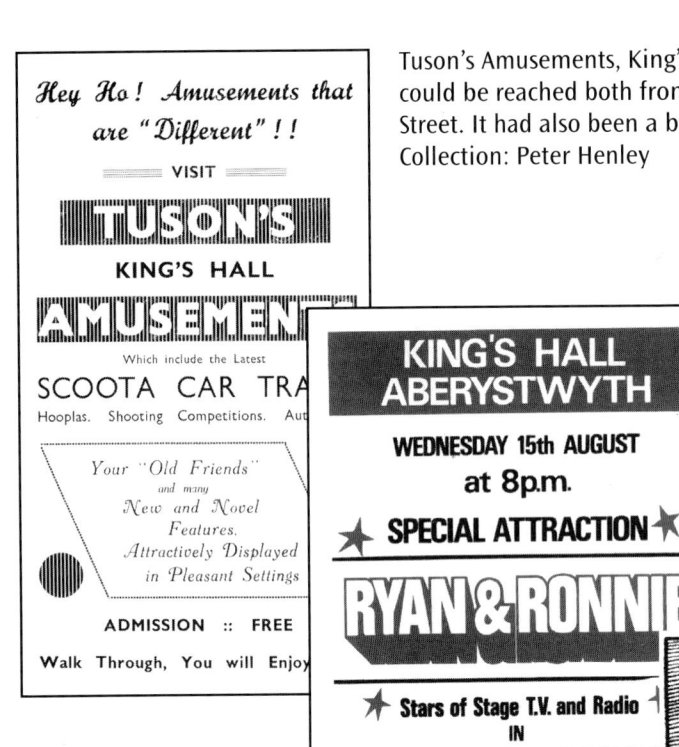

Tuson's Amusements, King's Hall. This basement funfair could be reached both from the promenade and Bath Street. It had also been a boxing booth in the 1940s.
Collection: Peter Henley

A poster advertising the popular Welsh Ryan and Ronnie duo, who performed in the King's Hall during the mid 1970s Olde Tyme Music Halls.
Collection: Peter Henley

A lively cartoon depicting the King's Hall and orchestra used on the front of summer show programmes during the 1950s. This one came from the *Zip a Hoy* show programme.
Collection: Peter Henley

DANCE BANDS

The 1920s were marked by an increased freedom in attitude to and awareness of dress and appearance, in a developing trend that broke away from the restrictive apparel of the Victorian and Edwardian eras. The quest for pleasure and music gelled with the new American vaudeville jazz rhythms and the inviting dance floors. The Charleston became the *in* dance, alongside the familiar strict tempos and the emerging Latin American dances. The gramophone competed with and contributed to the live music scene, offering the new sounds that came sooner to the most remote places. Locally, to initiate an interest in dancing, the Aberystwyth Dance Quartet was formed by Evered Davies.

EVERED DAVIES

Shortly after his return from France in 1918, at the end of the Great War, Evered Davies, a concert pianist and organist, ran a small band called *The Aberystwyth Dance Quartet*. The war had brought about many changes, one of which was Ragtime music. Evered, always keen to be in the forefront of popular music, had by now organised a collection of local musicians and created what he called a Dance Band. They advertised themselves in 1922 as a Syncopated Dance Orchestra and gained instant success with his new formation.

Evered became a major contributor to 20th century musical entertainment, both on the promenade, in the orchestra and in the dance hall. Although trained as a classical musician, Evered Davies and his band led the way in the world of light music locally between 1920 and 1940 and he became known as The Ambrose of Wales.

His *Syncopators* became the resident band on the pier from 1925 up to the outbreak of war in 1939, and he provided dance band music at the King's Hall, after its opening in 1935, and at countless other venues over Wales. He was appointed Director of Music in Aberystwyth in 1940 and conducted the Municipal Orchestra when the popularity of the light orchestra re-emerged in British resorts in the 1930s. This type of public entertainment on the promenade lasted until the late 1950s.

Evered drew from local talent and supported their training. One wax-moustached character, whose face can be seen in many of the town band photographs from the 1920s – 1940s, was Jack Jones, who played trumpet for Evered Davies. He lived in the house on the corner of Cambrian Street and Thespian Street and worked at Aberystwyth for the Great Western Railway.

In 1940, Evered Davies, as Musical Director, was invited to form a band for the summer season, at a cost of no more than £65 a week. It was made clear to him by the Borough Council Entertainments Committee: '*If any member of his band is called upon to serve in His Majesty's forces or terminates his services with the band, and that member is not a key man, or if he does not interfere with the efficiency of the band, then he should not be replaced.*' (*Cambrian News*, 16. 7. 1940)

BROADCASTING ON AUGUST 29th 1935

TUNE IN
WESTERN REGIONAL
WAVELENGTH
373.1 m.
at 9-45 p.m.

THIS POPULAR BAND IS AVAILABLE FOR WINTER ENGAGEMENTS AFTER OCTOBER 6th, 1935

All Communications
EVERED DAVIES
26 PIER STREET
ABERYSTWYTH
PHONE — — 641

EVERED DAVIES AND HIS BAND OF THE PIER BALLROOM ABERYSTWYTH

The era of the British dance band peaked during the 1930s along with the success of the radio. Television was still in its infancy when Evered Davies and his ballroom dance band were featured in a live broadcast on the *Western Regional Wavelength,* on BBC Radio, on August 29th, 1935. The production of an advertising postcard celebrated the event with a photograph of the band playing in the Pier Ballroom at Aberystwyth.

Photographer: Evered Davies.
Peter Henley collection.

A trumpet player who began his career with Evered's band is Ronnie Hughes. Ronnie lived in Penparcau and began lessons with Ralph Davies, Evered's son. Ronnie went on to become a top professional player, playing with many of the leading dance bands in Britain, in particular, Ted Heath's. Ronnie also excelled himself on the flugelhorn, an instrument not only well established in the brass band world, but also used as a solo instrument in big band recordings. It has similar pitch to the B flat trumpet but with a softer, warmer tone with the sonority of a tenor horn. Ronnie is also known for one of the recordings of the ITV *Coronation Street* theme.

Evered's son Ralph, saxophone and clarinet player, had, towards the latter days of Evered's leadership, played a significant role in the band's success. He had been introduced into the band at the age of nine, in 1925, by his father. Within a short time, he was playing solos on soprano saxophone and xylophone. The band had expanded from a four-piece in the 1920s, through several increases in line-up, until finally settling as a swinging, successful nine-piece in the 1940s. Ralph's input eventually led to the inevitable takeover and emergence of the Ralph Davies Band, with its distinctive modern sound of the 1940s. He entertained thousands in the years from 1936 -1956, excluding the intervening war years.

Music History

The Aberystwyth Dance Quartet. Its instigator, Evered Davies, is seen at the piano with fellow musicians Harold Sayer on violin and tenor banjo; Cornelius Richardes, the Saxophone player and trombonist; and Ned Lewis, the drummer. The photograph was taken in the Parish Hall, now the Castle Theatre, in 1920. This was Evered Davies' first band. He soon went on to form his Syncopated Dance Orchestra.

Collection: Mrs Violet Davies. Photograph: Evered Davies

Aber Prom

Ralph Davies created his own dance band of ten from a nucleus of players who had previously performed in his father's Evered Davies Band. With new arrangements of popular wartime favourites, including the Glenn Miller tunes, and the addition of new, talented players, he successfully introduced new sounds and rhythms to the keen dance-goers of the post war period. Ralph Davies led the band on saxophone and clarinet and became popular in Radio Wales productions of *Rali Gamp* and *Shwt mae Heno?* with Alun Williams, and Mai Jones on *Workers Playtime*. Mai Jones, incidentally, was the writer of the well known song, *'We'll keep a welcome in the hillsides'*.

Collection: Violet Davies. Photographer: Evered Davies

A portrait of Ralph Hicks Davies (1916-1990).

Collection: Violet Davies.
Photographer: Evered Davies

LES FRANCES' BAND

Les Frances, who came originally from Liverpool, met Ralph Davies during his RAF war service in the Far East. Through a common interest in music and his electronics skills, he joined the Evered Davies family business in Aberystwyth at the end of World War II, in 1945, as a radio engineer, and pianist in the popular Ralph Davies dance band. When Ralph retired, Les formed his own band with several of Ralph's players and was in demand for local concerts, pantomime and dances until the 1980s. Les was a brilliant arranger along with Jim Clements on saxophone. He devised a small, amplified, electronic keyboard that was attached to his piano in the 1960s, leading the way towards the use of electronically enhanced sounds. He continued providing a dance band in the pier and King's Hall into the 1970s. He later became chief technician in the University's Department of Physics electronics laboratories and took part in rocket research projects, studying the upper ionosphere, until his retirement.

THE GAIETY DANCE BAND

The Gaiety Dance Band was formed by Hughie Humphries of 34 Prospect Street in the 1930s and continued to provide dance music locally until the 1950s. His pre-war band line up consisted of six players, including a violinist and cellist, a saxophonist, two brass players, a trumpeter and trombonist, and, finally, himself on drums. In his later years, his formation often totalled just three players, a pianist and drummer with the occasional soloist wind player. Hughie was always the drummer and leader. He offered the services of the band with these words on his business card:

> Open for all engagements
> Satisfaction guaranteed
> Member of the British Legion.

He prided himself on his military background, and for many years he volunteered to act as mace-bearer for local civic parades and processions, dressed always in his immaculate uniform. Following the successful creation of the 1st Cadet Regimental Band of over fifty local boys from within the Cardiganshire Army Cadet Force, he became its drum major.

Music History

The Les Frances Band. Les Frances, playing piano, is accompanied on stage by vocalist Dilys Jones; Jimmy Clements; Cecil Hutchings on string bass; Leslie Lloyd and Ronnie White, during a Latin American rhythm dance.

Collection; Ceredigion Museum

Aber Prom

Hughie Humphries with his side drum.

Collection: Peter Henley.
Photographer unknown

POP GROUPS

THE NIGHT RIDERS

The post 1950s direction taken by popular music incorporated many new sounds and rhythms, which included Rock & Roll, the Twist and the Blues of Elvis Presley and Buddy Holly. The dress style of the post war era hung onto its formal mode alongside the changing attire of the pop groups, which ousted the dance band. The long-haired *Beatles*, in their dark, fitted suits, may have influenced the clothes of the young Aberystwyth members of the newly formed *Night Riders* pop group, which became successful locally from July 1961. Several other formations shared the limelight with them, including the *Zenons*.

Musically, long gone were Ragtime, Boogie-woogie, Jive and Skiffle. The sound of the new acoustic guitar and sound amplification had become established world-wide, forming the basis of future developments in popular music.

THE XENONS

In 1963, the *Xenons* were formed locally and joined the big-beat boom with their line-up of five players. Within a short time they were providing the Parish Hall Saturday night College hops with the emerging 1960s style of dance music. The original five included Roy Jones, an accountant's assistant, on rhythm guitar; Vivian Williams, a newspaper compositor, on bass guitar; David Heyward, a professional photographer, on lead guitar; Ray Philips, a weighing machine mechanic, was lead vocalist; and Stuart Masters, who was still at school, played drums.

They augmented their instrumental roles individually with vocal music. Although they had the opportunity to turn professional, they concentrated on local events, along with appearances on television, BBC Radio 1 spots, and recording. Their style changed in later years, deserting the big-beat and rock and roll image in exchange for quality harmony in ballad form, akin to the American *Beach Boys*. As players left the band to follow their careers, new members were recruited to take their place, from the 1960s into the 1980s.

Aber Prom

The 1960s *Night Riders* pop group.
John Humphreys; Peter Lydyard; Jeff Davies; Christopher Edwards; Barry Evans and Ernest Watson.

Photographer: Evered Davies & Son. Collection: Mrs Violet Davies

Music History

The *Xenons* band in 1963. Left to right: Roy Jones; Christopher Edwards; John Humphries; Vivian Williams; Peter Lydyard; Photographer: Pickford. Collection: Mrs Olga Edwards

Aber Prom

PUNCH AND JUDY

The hook-nosed, hunch-backed character we recognise as Punch in the ever popular seaside children's Punch and Judy show originated in Naples, in Italy, in the 14th century, where he was known as Pulcinella. The cowardly, garishly-dressed puppet became known as Punchinello, who had gained a wife, Joan, by the end of the 17th century, when they became known as Punch and Judy as they travelled through France and on to Britain. They became greatly loved and admired by all, especially by the famous Charles Dickens, who was fascinated by their antics in the famous show. His admiration of the pair was proved when he referred to them in his novel, *The Old Curiosity Shop*.

Aberystwyth promenade visitors, young and old, shared in the delights of Punch and Judy. An early photograph, taken about 1910, shows a Punch and Judy stand being erected near the old lifeboat slipway. Punch and Judy booths appear in photographs taken

A festival of Punch and Judy entertainment was held on Aberystwyth promenade in August 2004, continuing on from the success of a previous event in 2003. A member for over 40 years of the College of Punch and Judy Professors is Professor Glyn Edwards, who became active in 1962, when he was the youngest performer at the unveiling of the plague to Mr Punch in Covent Garden. He and his wife Mary, a notable puppeteer, have travelled the world giving shows. Glyn, who regards himself as a Punch and Judy activist, has written books, directed TV programmes and provided training in the skills of working Punch and Judy. Glyn considers Mr Punch to be one of world drama's great comic creations, whose story has a wealth of meaning for each generation who comes to it.

Extracts from 'Punch & Judy College of Professors' web site.
Photography: Peter Henley

A summertime beach performance of Punch & Judy on Marine Terrace proved to be a great attraction for all ages, during an early Edwardian summer. In contrast to the large audience, one boy appears unimpressed as he walks away from the spellbound crowd. Photographer unknown. Collection: Ceredigion Museum

Aber Prom

on the promenade in the early 20th century, and in 1948, when Fred and Dora Rayne produced shows on the promenade. (Official Guide 1948, Ceredigion Museum 1985.11.1)

In 1987, the 325th anniversary of Mr Punch's 'official' birthday was celebrated nationwide. The Welsh celebration took place at Aberystwyth and was organised by Professor Bill Dane, who has lent his collection of puppets to Ceredigion Museum.

A recent revival in the show's popularity was supported by the Town Council and culminated in a festival of Punch and Judy on the promenade during the August bank holidays in the new Millennium.

During the summer months of the 1970s, Mike Wallis and his wife staged and directed several variety shows in the King's Hall, plus children's shows on the promenade, including the well known Punch and Judy in 1976.

Photography: Peter Henley

Punch and Judy

During the 2004 Punch & Judy Festival held in Aberystwyth, several booths were erected in the bandstand, on the slipway and in the Ceredigion Museum in Terrace Road. The left hand booth in the photograph was provided by Tony Clarke, whose first show was in Gorleston-on-Sea in 1976. He is a second generation Punch and Judy man, being the son of Bryan Clarke, who also entertained at Aberystwyth. The right hand booth was run by Brian and Alison Davey, who are resident summer performers at Lyme Regis, in Dorset. They perform at festivals throughout the UK and overseas and their stage name is The Puppetree Company. They also make and supply stage and film props etc. for the entertainment industry.

Collection & Photography: Peter Henley

BATHING

> **SEA BATHING FOR THE WORKING CLASSES PARTIES AVAILING THEMSELVES OF THE TRAINS WILL BE ENABLED TO BATHE AND REFRESH THEMSELVES IN AMPLE TIME TO ATTEND A PLACE OF WORSHIP**

Although advice suggesting that good health could be achieved by sea bathing was given in the United Kingdom in the 17th century, the most publicised early acceptance must have been when the London press announced on Saturday, July 7th, 1789: *'Think but of the surprise of his Majesty when at the first time of bathing he had no sooner popped his royal head under the water than a band of music concealed in a neighbouring bathing machine struck up: God save great George, Our King.'*

It detailed the response by George III to his physician's advice to enter the waves in a ceremonial plunge at Weymouth. That historic attempt to stem his declining health became a turning point in seaside interest. The King's public immersion tempted those to follow suit who previously may not have considered even visiting the seaside. The suggestion of bathing in the sea became, in reality, an adventure rather than, as initially suggested, a health-seeking practice. The practice blossomed and became incorporated into the inimitable trip to the coast. The Lancashire & Yorkshire Railway Company advertised in 1840:

To overcome the shyness of the more modest bather, the bathing machine, originally popularized by the Prince Regent in the 1820s, appeared in the form of a horse-drawn, wooden hut on wheels that could be eased up to the shoreline and offer the bather the combined act of changing and bathing in relative privacy, i.e. in through the front door and out into the sea via the back door.

As the numbers of bathing machines increased it became necessary and prudent to keep male and female bathing at separate ends of resort beaches. In some larger British resorts, an authorised patrolman on horseback would oversee the situation and prevent mixed bathing, and fines were imposed on those flouting the rules. In Aberystwyth, one rather irate female bather wrote to the *Cambrian News* in 1905, complaining that men had been seen swimming far too close to the women's bathing machines.

Bathing increased in popularity after that pioneering Georgian period. Bathing huts appeared at Aberystwyth in 1801, and by 1826 there were 21 available on the beach. During the peak of seaside popularity, in the Victorian Jubilee year of 1887, there were 73 to be seen on the north and south beaches. It became difficult for families arriving on the promenade and having to split up to conform to the segregation rule. The honour fell to Bexhill-on-Sea for introducing British mixed bathing in 1901, which arrangement was quickly followed in other resorts. Resorts began advertising the new facility nationally. By the 1930s, the numbers of bathing machines declined and all were withdrawn within that decade as bathing habits were liberalised. The main family names associated locally with bathing machine hire, for several generations, were: the Evanses, at the turn of the century; then, the Lewises and Whites. One of the last to provide a service was Leslie Lewis, who also played a tuba in the town band on the promenade during the 1920s. The only link with that bathing hut period survived on the beach until the 1960s, in the form of a stone drinking trough for the horses. It stood against the promenade beach wall, below the old lifeboat capstan.

A steadfast occupant of a seaside bathing machine is depicted in this comic postcard from 1906. Collection: Peter Henley

Aber Prom

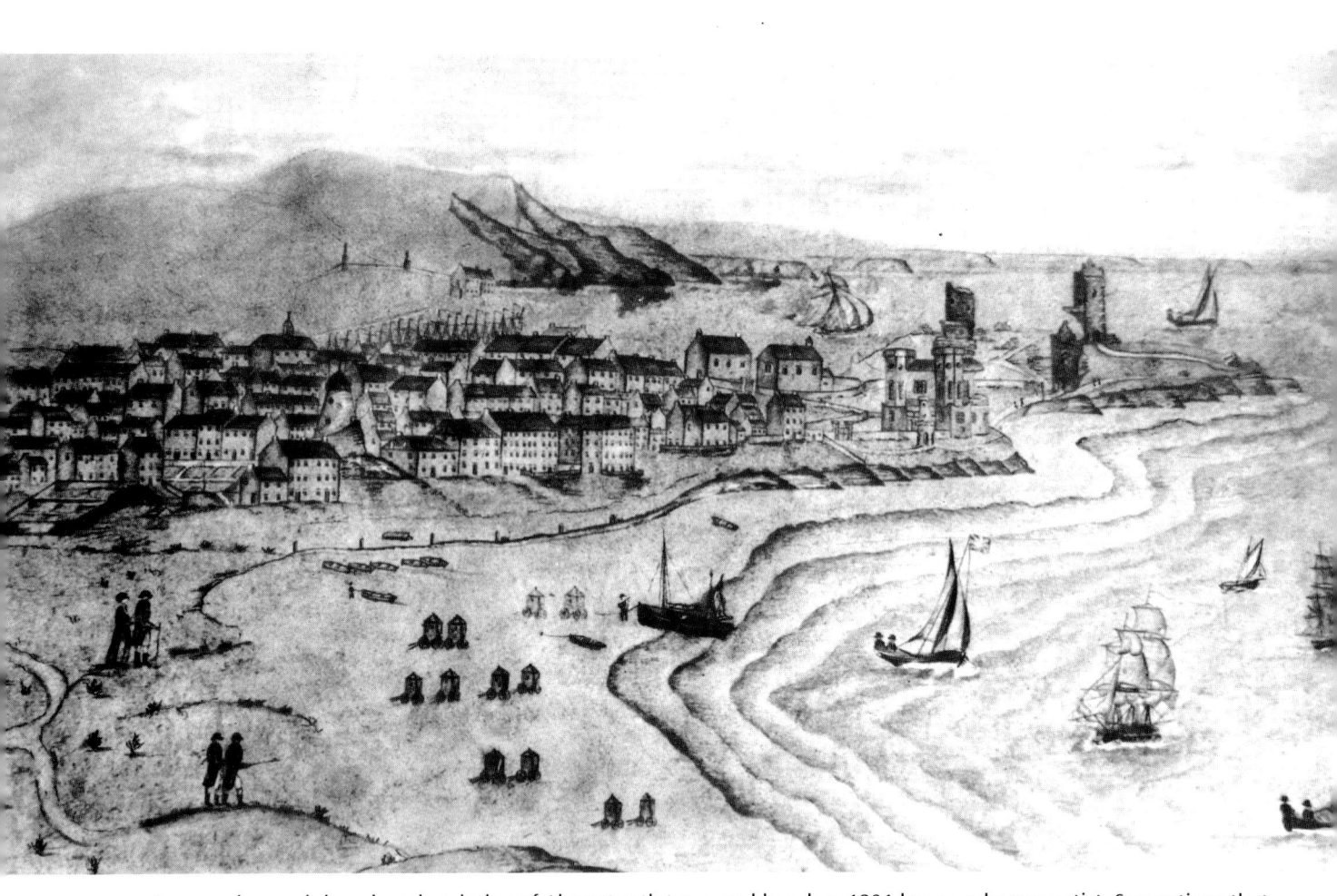

A monochrome ink and wash painting of Aberystwyth town and beach c. 1801 by an unknown artist. Suggestions that modest bathing was taking place are heralded by the appearance of bathing machines on the beach and what was probably a pleasure sailing boat at the water's edge. Lewis Collection, National Library of Wales.

Bathing machines on Aberystwyth beach opposite Marine Terrace, in an Edwardian summer at the turn of the 20th century. Collection: Peter Henley. Photographer: Emile Thomas Evans

A cartoon depicting a Lewis bathing machine in 1901. *'Now mind, if any of those nasty people with cameras come near, you're to send them away!'*

Collection: Bill Pertwee, from Punch, September 1901.

A happy group of young bathers in period costume helping to haul in their boat c. 1900.

Collection: Ceredigion Museum.
Photographer unknown.

During the 1960s, the Aberystwyth Town Council provided six children's trampolines on the beach, in an enclosure created near the old lifeboat capstan.

Collection: Ceredigion Library

Although local sea angling is far more successful off shore, many varieties of fish are caught from the beach: bass, pollack, dogfish, conger eel and the ever popular, seasonal, mackerel. Frequent offshore landings are also made of skate, codling and gurnard. Sightings near the shore have been made of rather larger specimens, such as sunfish, basking shark and monkfish. The lone fisherman in the photograph was candidly captured by the camera near the southern end of the promenade, opposite the harbour. Photography: Peter Henley

Aber Prom

DONKEYS

Donkey rides have been regarded as synonymous with seaside attractions at British seaside resorts for about 150 years. The small but strong, willing donkeys offered an unforgettable experience to the very young; etching that first ride forever in their memories. Leather-saddled and bridled for the day's duty, the gentle-natured animals assured a safe passage along the promenade. Their presence locally is noted from at least 1860 until the present day. In the summer of 1901 there were four owners offering rides: Mrs Jane Jones of Llangawsai, Mrs Eliza Morgan, Mrs David Morgan and Mrs White. The Corporation allowed them a maximum of five donkeys each, to be used for rides.

During the mid 20th century, the main summer donkey-owner was affectionately known as Jack Price the Donkeys. He was born in 1873, in 28 Portland Road, Aberystwyth, of a Llanafan family. He was well known between the wars for his sightseeing, charabanc rides to Devil's Bridge from a pitch near the Railway Station. He will be remembered principally for his promenade donkey rides during the summer months, from 1912 to the 1950s, when he was in his eighties. During those latter years, the cost of a ride from opposite the entrance to Terrace Road to the slipway was three-pence (1.25p).

An added attraction of his included a four-wheeled cart, suitable for four children, hauled by a single donkey along the promenade in front of the Royal Belle Vue Hotel. Overnight, the docile Connemara donkeys were kept at the rear of West Wales Garage (now Cambrian Tyres) in Loveden Road. The donkeys, followed either by Jack, with his leather money satchel around his neck, or his daughter Myfanwy, known as Fanw, en route to the stable, would pause outside the Crystal Palace public house in Queen's road, and wait for the landlord to appear, with a treat of bread for them. Jack Price sometimes kept them grazing on Pen Dinas, or near the golf links. On one occasion, a donkey collapsed and died in Chalybeate Street. A policeman happened to pass and thought that the incident ought to be recorded, but he couldn't spell Chalybeate, and so he had the donkey dragged into the adjacent Queen's Street, which he could spell. Over the years, Jack gained a special understanding with his animals and never had to resort to the stick.

The Welsh magazine 'Y Cymro' remembered him on September 26th, 1952, in the following rhyme:

'O na bydda'n haf o hyd
Rasus mulod round y byd
Bromenad Aberystwyth gyda mulod
I'r plant ers deugan mlynedd'

Translation:
'Oh that it would be forever summer
Donkey races around the world
Aberystwyth promenade with donkeys
For the children over forty years'

Donkeys

The family of the former Gwalia Garage in North Parade, with Jack Price's donkey and cart, opposite Ashley's Hotel and the King's Hall in 1939.

Photographer: Maurice Henley. Collection: Peter Henley

Aber Prom

Jack Price in his later years, in 1952, with 3-year-old Brenda Haines, who lives locally. He told Brenda, "I am going to carry on for ever."

(*Cambrian News,* 3. 10. 2005).
Collection: National Library of Wales.
Photographer: Geoff Charles

Donkeys

John Vaughan on the promenade with three of his donkeys in 2004. Following the retirement of Jack Price, the provision of donkey rides was taken over by the Vaughan family of Llanidloes, in 1955. The original operators were two brothers, John and Tommy Vaughan. Tommy died a few years ago, and John has retired from the business. His nephew, also named John, is seen here with three of his faithful donkeys, ready for the day's rides on Marine Terrace. The donkeys were bred locally and spend their rest hours happily grazing on the slopes of Pen Dinas.

Collection & Photographer: Peter Henley

Aber Prom

PLEASURE BOATS

Although the towns along the Cardigan Bay coastline have been associated with shipping for many centuries, the era of the pleasure boat is synonymous with the modern development of coastal resorts, particularly at Aberystwyth. From the 18th century, sketches and paintings exist of the town and include shore-line vessels that would have been involved both in sea fishing and the tourist trade. The boat owners would have responded to the interests of the pioneering visitors, from the late 1700s, and in doing so, initiated a trade that continues to this day.

STEAMERS

By 1842 a substantial steam vessel had been built. The S.S. *Plynlimon* offered a passenger-carrying service between Aberystwyth, Bristol and Liverpool, which survived into the late 1860s. Weekly trips were also advertised to Pwllheli and Bardsey Island, off the Llyn peninsula. The ship was owned by the Aberystwyth and Aberdovey Steam Packet Company. Its Master was Captain William Wraight and its Company Agent Henry Culliford. An article in the *Aberystwyth Observer* of July 30th, 1859 stated: 'The steamer Plynlimon *was dispatched on a pleasure trip to Bardsey Island. It started at 9.30 in the morning with upwards of eighty excursionists, having a band of music on board. After landing at the place of destination, the company went in pursuit of their various amusements, and about five 'o'clock they re-embarked and returned shortly after ten o' clock that evening.'*

By the turn of the 20th century, there were four steam vessels plying for trade off the beach: *May, Lizzie, Snowdon* and *Solent*. The *Lizzie* was the only screw and sail steamer to be built at Aberystwyth, and she was launched on the south beach at *Ro Fawr* by I Hopkins in 1886. (*Cambrian News,* July 1859). The *Snowdon* was owned by Morgan Owen and David Lloyd of Baker Street, and to ease tension amongst the boat owners, the town council, in 1889, refused permission for the *Snowdon*'s owners to place an advertising board on the beach, which had created an unfair trading situation.

The pleasure boat boom began in 1914, before the start of the Great War, providing a summer income for local boatmen. The huge influx of day trippers pouring onto the promenade and beach provided a guaranteed summer occupation for them, with queues of prospective passengers lining up daily for a trip around the bay.

A special meeting was held on July 25th, 1913, in response to letters from irate visitors complaining that the pleasure boats were overcrowded and that passengers were being overcharged. A number of boatmen attended the meeting and faced further accusations of operating their boats on Sundays.

The owner of the motor boat *Mauritania* that operated from the beach at Marine Terrace was later fined £2 plus costs for overcrowding his boat.

Pleasure Boats

The pleasure steamer *May* discharging it's passengers at Aberystwyth beach in the late 19th century. The screw propelled vessel was powered by a small steam engine, hence the funnel to take away the smoke and steam. During very hot spells of weather, a frilled canvas awning would be erected on poles over the stern area, to allow passengers to sit in the shade. A normal complement of crew and passengers would be fewer than twenty. The skipper and crew would invite visitors to board at the beach and partake of journeys to Aberdovey at 2.00 p.m., return fare three shillings (15p), or to Monk's Cave at 6.30 p.m. for two shillings (10p).

Collection: Ceredigion Museum. Photographer unknown

Aber Prom

A delightfully peaceful summer's day at the close of the 19th century, with little more than a ripple on the sea's surface. The carvel-built pleasure boat *Victory* awaits custom as the *Maggie*, under full sail and oars, on a falling tide, leaves with a boatful of passengers. One of the rowing boats on the beach belonged to John Brodigan of Trefechan and was licensed to carry four passengers.

Collection: Peter Henley. Photographer: Emile Thomas Evans

Pleasure Boats

A rather overcrowded *Mauritania*, discharging its passengers onto Aberystwyth beach in the early 1900s.
Photographer: William Jenkins. Collection: Ceredigion Museum 1985.24.66

Aber Prom

Although many visitors travelled to the resort on Sundays, the chance of a trip in the bay was thwarted by a local clergyman, Rev'd William Jones, in 1890, when he successfully prevented the local boatmen from plying for trade on the holy day. Although their business may not exactly have been a profane act, the ban became long-standing and restricted Sunday boating until 1935, when a plebiscite of townspeople voted in favour of a return of the service after a break of 45 years.

(Aberystwyth Town Council minutes 20.5.1890, 3.6.1890)

By the 1930s, screw-propelled, passenger-carrying boats were being operated from the beach. A regular quintet of vessels, whose names became synonymous with Aberystwyth, appeared regularly, although, in 1936, there were nine registered vessels plus thirteen rowing boats. Licences taken by the watermen during the season amounted to 48. The beach inspector's report on the state of boating in that year concluded: *'It gives me great pleasure to report that all the boatmen conducted themselves satisfactorily, there being no shouting or touting.'*

Five of the regularly seen pleasure boats are as follows:

BIRMINGHAM CITY

The pleasure boat *Birmingham City* was built at Appledore, in Devon, and was commissioned in 1924 by Captain John Rees (1868-1937) of Anwylfan, Dinas Terrace. He served as master of this motor launch, plying for trade off the beach alongside six similar well-known vessels, during the summer months of the 1920s and 1930s. He offered trips around the bay, including afternoon visits to Aberdovey. The launch's claim to fame was that it was the first diesel-powered pleasure boat to work at Aberystwyth.

Captain Rees first went to sea at Aberystwyth when he was aged 13, and he retired in 1937, as a Master Mariner, having accomplished 102 sail and steam, worldwide voyages during his service in the Merchant Navy and on WW1 Special Service 'Q' ships in the Royal Naval Reserve. Following his retirement, he returned to Aberystwyth, to serve the public with his well maintained pleasure boat, *Birmingham City*. It later served as a ferry at Neyland, near Milford Haven, in Pembrokeshire.

(Information: Frank Collison of Sandal, West Yorkshire)

WILD ROSE

The *Wild Rose*, a much smaller vessel, was owned by Jack Davies and Evan Jones of Aberystwyth.

WORCESTER CASTLE

The largest of the familiar pleasure boats of the 1930s was the petrol-engine, twin screw *Worcester Castle*. It was built at Appledore, on the North Devon Coast, and was owned by Captain Brown of Aberystwyth.

MAURETANIA

The sleek lines of the clipper-bowed pleasure and fishing boat *Mauretania* became a very familiar site on the shore at Aberystwyth during the early decades of the 20th century. It was owned by the long-serving

Pleasure Boats

Pleasure boats plying for trade at Aberystwyth beach c. 1924. They are: Left to right: *Wild Rose, Worcester Castle, Pride of the Midlands, Birmingham City* and *Mauretania*.

Collection: Ceredigion Museum 1980.7.11. Photographer unknown

former coxswain of the RNLI lifeboat, David Williams, and Harry Davies. (Information: David E Jenkins, *The passing of a Port,* 1980.)

Although the above boats were serviceable at the onset of World War II, in 1939, no boats from Aberystwyth were involved in the Dunkirk evacuation, but the *Worcester Castle* and the *Pride of the Midlands* were commandeered during the early 1940s, and sailed in company to Holyhead. The *Worcester Castle* stayed there, and became involved in the saving of a blazing oil tanker. The other, the *Pride of the Midlands,* continued on to Liverpool, where she was placed on a lorry and taken to the Firth of Clyde. Both survived the war and returned afterwards to Aberystwyth to continue their pleasure boat activities. (CM 1988.46.1)

The Davies family of the High Street sea food business survived for over 100 years. Its most popular shop was at 1 Great Darkgate Street, which Albert Davies ran for many years. The 1930s family-run boat that offered trips locally was called the *Belle-Isle.*

PRIDE OF THE MIDLANDS

The attraction of the seaside extended to a trip around the bay, words that would be called out from the promenade and beach for many summers, by the boatmen. One person in particular who hailed the holidaymakers with an invitation to climb aboard, in the 1950s, was the unforgettable George White of the White Brothers trio, well known for their sturdy and capable pleasure boat, the *Pride of the Midlands,* built in 1925. The brothers, Ben, Billy and George, came from a family from Crynfryn Buildings; they began operating from the central beach opposite the King's Hall in the summer months of the 1930s. Billy, the engineer, and George, the ticket salesman, lived in Portland Road, and, Ben, the skipper, in Thespian Street, and later in Terrace Road, where he had a fishmonger's shop. A large display board would be erected on the promenade alongside the old lifeboat capstan, advertising the capabilities of the pleasure boat and its fares. It was described as:

> 'A FAST AND POWERFUL
> TWIN SCREW
> PASSENGER MOTOR YACHT'
>
> THE PRIDE OF THE MIDLANDS
>
> THE LAST WORD IN COMFORT
> AND CONVENIENCE
>
> BUILT UNDER THE PERSONAL
> SUPERVISION OF HIS MAJESTY'S
> INSPECTORS
>
> TRIPS IN THE BAY 4 SHILLINGS

Pleasure Boats

WHITE BROS. Motor Boat Proprietors
——— Aberystwyth ———

Fast up-to-date Motor Ships. "Pride of the Midlands" and "Worcester Castle." Registered Board of Trade Capacity of Boats up to 300 passengers. Modern conveniences and wet weather accommodation. Available for sea trips in Cardigan Bay, 1 or 2 hours. Also afternoon trips to Aberdovey, 20 miles return sea trip, landing for 1 hour. Special quotations for Parties.
Write: Proprietors.

1931 *'White Brothers motor boat proprietors'* for the *'Pride of the Midlands'* and *'Worcester Castle'* pleasure boats.

(From the 1931 Aberystwyth Guide)

Ben White and his mate would take the trippers as far as Clarach and back, or for an afternoon trip to Aberdovey, or south to Monk's Cave below Blaenplwyf. The trippers would board the vessel from the beach by walking up a wooden gangway, which would be hauled up into position onto the bow.

At the end of the afternoons, it was possible for local lads to get a free trip to the harbour, when the vessel was en route to its overnight moorings. When Ben White became the surviving brother, he decided to invest in a smaller pleasure boat and sold the *Pride* (as it was affectionately known) to a company operating on the Thames in London. It left Aberystwyth manned by a small crew and with sufficient fuel to last the week-long journey around the south coast of Britain. One of the crew, Reg White of Greenfield Street, who was also a musician with the Ralph Davies band, recalled how the *Pride* was safely delivered to its intended operating quay near Westminster Bridge, in the 1960s. Not long after, its new life was sadly curtailed when it became entangled with an underwater obstacle near Tower Bridge and sank, becoming a total loss.

Ben White, the last of the boating family, died in August 1978, aged 82 years. He had been the proud owner of both the *Pride of the Midlands* and the *Worcester Castle* from 1925-1968. A previous owner of the *Worcester Castle* had been Captain John Brown of High Street. He had formerly been a master with the Mathias family of Aberystwyth ship-owners.

Other well known boating families included the Parrys and the Daniels of High Street. The Parry Brothers, Danny and Billy, owned a popular pleasure boat, the *Seahawk*, following the Second World War in the 1940s. (Extract from: Aberystwyth Yesterday exhibition.)

Many smaller boats would appear on the beach during peak periods, offering trips, especially when a visiting warship was anchored off the promenade. A change in the passenger-carrying safety regulations nationally, following a boating tragedy near Penmaenpool in the 1960s, saw a decline in the pleasure boating trade locally.

Following the Second World War, several boats, including an ex RAF rescue boat renamed the *Estelle*, offering exhilarating high speed rides, continued to offer rowing and motor boat trips.

Regardless of the provision of a new landing stage in the mid 1980s, the decline in the number of pleasure boats working from the main beach continued and the service finally ceased in 1990.

ROWING BOATS

The more adventurous visitors took a rowing boat trip in the bay, to admire the views and the sea birds or to catch fish. The boats would be rowed by their owners, the local seamen, usually for an hour's outing.

On 17th August 1798, Captain Frederick Jones stayed in Aberystwyth and recorded in his diary that he took: '...*a boat to Towyn with Mrs Jones, Mr Lewis of Yatt, his two nieces, Mrs and Miss Hooper of Herefordshire. ...out all night in an open boat on ye sea...*'

Pleasure Boats

One of the last of the pleasure boats to operate from the beach at Aberystwyth was the *Bounty,* owned and operated by Ben White. Following the sale of the *Pride of the Midlands,* he invested in a smaller boat. Ably assisted by Billy Parry, he plied for trade, offering trips around the bay at the height of the summer. During the infrequent visits by naval warships, Ben would be overwhelmed by trippers and locals keen to inspect the ship off shore at close quarters. One such visiting warship, seen in the photograph, was the Royal Navy's destroyer HMS *Defender* that anchored in the bay during an official visit in July 1969. It was one of the Royal Navy's Daring class destroyers and had played the part of a cruiser as one of the last of the conventional gun destroyers built for the Royal Navy. It was built in July 1950 at Stephens' yards, near Govan, Glasgow, in Scotland, with a displacement of 3,820 tons and a length of 390 feet (118 metres). When in commission, it had a complement of between 270 and 290 men. It was decommissioned in 1972. One vessel of its class survives in the Peruvian Navy.

Collection & Photographer: Peter Henley

Ben White and mate, Billy Parry, are seen preparing to depart from Aberystwyth beach in July 1969, on board the pleasure boat *Bounty*.

Collection & Photograph: Peter Henley

Aber Prom

A 1930s view of a row of small pleasure and fishing boats tied up to the promenade slipway. The AB26 *Belle Isle* passengers are disembarking by crossing over the AB46 *Emerald Star* and the AB11 *Swanee,* to get to land.

Collection: Aberystwyth Town Library

The fabric of the promenade has benefited from grant-aided improvements, which included resurfacing of the promenade deck in the 1990s, facade maintenance and, in the 1980s, a replacement boat slipway. Unfortunately, the timing of its construction in quality teak and greenheart timber, and the removal of its time served predecessor, did not coincide with any sustained pleasure boating. Its intention, assuming it was to support local boat owners, never came to fruition; its completion occurring some time after the cessation of launching from Marine Terrace. Its sole purpose today appears to be limited to 'wave dodging' by young people. The platform at the landward end supports a ceremonial mast, which was removed during the modification, but was reinstated following a plea by the Aberystwyth Civic Society.

Photography: Peter Henley

Pleasure Boats

The following day, they returned by foot and the ferry at Ynyslas. Not surprisingly, this appears to have been very irresponsible, and no mention is made of how the boat was returned to Aberystwyth. (Oliver, R.C.B. (1968), Holidays at Aberystwyth, 1798-1823 in 'Ceredigion' Volume x, No. 3)

Generally, the rowing boats would be launched directly off the beach, although the slipway was available for boarding during suitable tide conditions. The harbour was not normally considered suitable for pleasure boat hire. Many local boating family names could be recognised painted onto the stern board of their boats. Of the seventy available for hire, one rowing boat in particular, in 1910, was owned by John Brodigan, whose family had been closely linked with the RNLI locally. The boat was licensed to carry four passengers.

Of the thousands of boat trips taken from Aberystwyth, most must have been enjoyable, but there were a few people who had bad experiences. For example, in April 1914, some students rowed to Egg Rock and Monk's Cave, a few miles south of the harbour, on a clear morning. The wind strengthened and they became exhausted while trying to row back. Fortunately, friends called out the lifeboat and they were rescued.

The local Corporation were forced to pass bye-laws, appoint an inspector and grant licences to those responsible boat owners, during the hey-day of boating. The condition of the boats would have been considered a priority. It was possible to hire a rowing boat from the beach as late as the 1950s, although the number of boats had dwindled to no more than five by then.

A typically large number of rowing boats for hire on Aberystwyth beach c.1900. The lack of boats afloat probably coincided with it being a little too choppy to launch the lightweight craft.

**Collection: Peter Henley.
Photographer unknown**

THE UNIVERSITY ROWING CLUBS

The University Ladies' Rowing Club was formed in 1891. Rowing had become one of the most popular outdoor activities by 1921 and employed its own boatman to oversee and train the students in the skills of rowing and swimming. One particular local seafarer, Jackie Williams, was known to all as 'Jackie the boatman'. He referred to the club members as his young ladies, and he was considered a veritable mine of information and an unquestionable authority on all things connected with the sea.

In 1919, the University Ladies' Swimming Club was formed. Not one of the members would be allowed into the sea without Jackie's presence.

The men's club had been formed during the early days of the University, probably in the 1870s. Until 1885, the college had only one rowing boat, named *Otter*. In the same year, a new boat, named *Antigone*, was bought, helped by the £3.50 proceeds of a College Musical Society production of Antigone. The next boat acquired, in 1891, was named *Cymru Fydd*. (Free Wales) and, by 1893, the Aberystwyth Borough Council had granted the College free use of a boat shed.

FISHING BOATS

Sea-fishing and sailing are probably the oldest surviving occupations linking man with the abundance of food available in the waters of Cardigan Bay. Observers on shore in later days would have seen numerous fishing boats plying for trade along the coast. The abundance of herring in the bay attracted many to trawl and land their catches locally. One particular type of vessel seen, with a distinctive rig, was known as the Morecambe Bay prawner or nobbie. With their attractive sloping sterns and simple sails, they would often moor off Aberystwyth promenade, to dry their sails. The crews would fish in the Irish Sea and bring their haul to several of the small harbours along the bay, during the summer months, before returning to their home bases in the autumn.

The University of Wales Aberystwyth Ladies' Rowing Club group with Jackie Williams, the boatman, about 1920, outside the College main entrance in King Street.

Collection: Peter Henley. Photographer: H H Davies

Morecambe bay fishing boats moored near Aberystwyth pier c. 1900.

Photographer: Emile Thomas Evans

PHOTOGRAPHERS

In the 1920s, many holidaymakers would have brought the family box camera with them and, no doubt, would have relied on local photographic studio shops to develop and print their black and white snapshots. The place to go, of course, would have been Pier Street where there were a number of studios. As early as July 1860, an advert in the *Aberystwyth Observer and Cardiganshire General Advertiser* offered a photographic service and invited sitters to visit their studio to have their photograph taken.

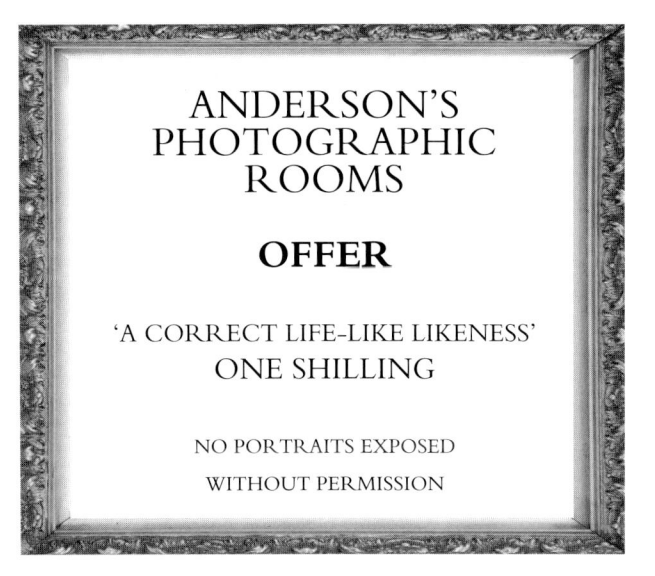

> ## ANDERSON'S PHOTOGRAPHIC ROOMS
>
> ### OFFER
>
> 'A CORRECT LIFE-LIKE LIKENESS'
> ONE SHILLING
>
> NO PORTRAITS EXPOSED
> WITHOUT PERMISSION

The Victorian and Edwardian generations of Aberystwyth photographers mostly operated from Pier Street. The earliest of these 19th century professionals was Ebenezer Morgan, who operated from 1857 until 1901. Successive studios were later run by Gyde, from 1875 to 1917, who was followed by his son-in-law, Hubert George Pickford, and his grandson, Glyn Pickford. Pickford senior became the first photographer in the town to use electric light in his studio, thus dispensing with the use of body clamps and head restrainers to keep the sitter still during the long camera exposures.

Next door, Henry Hicks Davies (1862-1943) traded in a similar fashion. H H, as he was known, had been a champion Welsh swimmer in his youth. Aged six weeks, he arrived in Aberystwyth by ship, in 1862, from Haverfordwest. His son Evered (1889-1964) established himself in later life as a highly respected musician and businessman. His shop in Pier Street became a Mecca for the serious music lover and photographer. He was later to become the official college photographer. He was joined in business by his son Ralph (1916-1990), who also went on to become a professional musician and photographer. The Davies family made a significant contribution to the success of photography and modern music in Wales.

Some of the other local photographers practising in the first half of the 20th century were William Jenkins, Frank Culliford, Emile Thomas Evans and Arthur J Lewis. Yesterday, they unwittingly opened for us and for those of tomorrow, a window on a vanished world; their captured moment in time.

Aber Prom

Sample photographic packets in which customers snaps and negatives would be placed ready for collection from the town photography shops.

Collection: Peter Henley

BEACH PHOTOGRAPHERS

Beach photographers, up until the 1940s, relied on selling their work to the day tripper, with emphasis placed on the 'instant portrait' and processing film on a 'while you wait' basis, or, at least, as William Jenkins would have offered: Ready in one day.

The early beach photographers would have had a portable means of developing an image within a few minutes, either in a convenient, wheeled darkroom or a cleverly concealed arrangement fitted below the camera tripod. The result was described as a tin-type, an image produced on a durable metal plate. Often the cost would be about 6 pence in pre-decimal currency. (Part detail from: Website of David Simkin on the History of Brighton beach photographers)

One form of commercial activity that appears to have been allowed on the promenade was beach photography. The only known photographer to work in this way was William Jenkins, known locally as Will Nell. During the first half of the 20th century, he stood on the promenade and beach and invited people to pose, to allow him to 'take their likenesses'. He was able to develop the tin-type in a set of tanks, possibly slung under the camera tripod and hidden from the light by his camera drape, although other photographs, taken in a conventional way, using glass plates, would be processed back at his studio and delivered to the customer within a day. His studio and darkrooms were in 32, Little Darkgate Street, which is now named Eastgate Street. Very few of his 'instant' portraits or groups are known to have survived, although there are examples of his studio work preserved.

He was also a town bandsman, playing the tenor horn. His face can be seen in many group photographs of the town band, and the Cardigan Militia Band, from the early years of the century until the 1930s. He was also a Welsh-speaking member of the now lost Shiloh Chapel, in North Parade. He taught children in Sunday school in Skinner Street's Ebenezer Chapel, now also demolished.

The Visitors
Photographer
JENKINS
32
Little Dark Gate S
BEAUTIFULLY FINISHED POST-CARD
Unlimited Testimonials daily from Visitors
Highest Quality of work at Popular Prices
NOTE — Ready in One Day.

Photographers

William Jenkins, beach photographer of Aberystwyth c. 1880-1950, known locally as Will Nell. He offered a photographic service, inviting patrons the opportunity to record all manner of subjects. His studio was at 32, Little Darkgate Street, now called Eastgate Street. He also produced and sold his work in the form of local view cards. He proudly advertised himself as 'The Visitors Photographer' and claimed that he would have the results of his work ready in one day

The photographer of this picture of William Jenkins was William Hammond, who came from Stalybridge, Cheshire, to live in Criccieth. He took on the running of a general store and photographic business. He practiced from 1911 until 1965. Collection: National Library of Wales

A typical Edwardian, saucy, seaside comic postcard with the caption *'Snap Shots at the Seaside – Got 'Em',* sent from Aberystwyth on August 8th, 1906.

FOOD

SEAFOOD

There would have been numerous restaurants and cafeterias within the town, to provide the large numbers of summer visitors with daily meals. On the promenade and beach, apart from table sittings offered by the hotels, it would have been possible to buy outdoors ready-made light refreshments, snacks, fruit and the ever popular ice cream. Alternatively, from the large number of local fishing boats, regular supplies of freshly caught fish, crabs and lobsters were always available, and for many years, especially in the early years of tourism, it was possible to buy fresh fish and shellfish: periwinkle, oyster, whelk, mussel and cockle. The periwinkles, found in abundance on local rocks at low tide, were easy to gather and would be transported in sacks on the backs of the collectors. They would be washed in fresh water, lightly boiled and sold from small promenade huts. Unlike many shellfish, the periwinkle (*Littorina littorea*) is regarded today as one of the few feeders on seaweed that does not absorb high levels of toxins. The other shellfish, which do not appear in sufficient commercial numbers here, would probably have arrived by train from the Whitstable mud flats in north Kent, or from Penclawdd in south Wales. The stalls, in the locality of the bandstand, survived until the 1930s.

A solitary cart with a woman probably selling fish near the old Lifeboat capstan on Marine Terrace c.1890.

Collection: Ceredigion Museum. Photographer unknown

During the mid-summer months, the catches of herring and mackerel daily landed at Aberystwyth could be bought from handcarts, on the promenade and in the town. Popular sellers included Lucy Wheeler, Marged y Pond, Mrs Thomas of Colenzo House and Ernie Meredith.

The photograph, taken by local photographer Arthur Lewis, shows Mrs Thomas of Colenzo House, Rheidol Terrace, selling mackerel from her iron-wheeled fish cart on South Marine Terrace, about 1925.

Collection: National Library of Wales. Photographer: Arthur Lewis

ICE CREAM VENDORS

The date when ice cream was first sold locally is uncertain. Its origins as we know it today began in the USA in 1846, when the first hand-cranked freezer was invented by a Nancy Johnson. It is also believed that the Chinese had previously developed the idea and, at one point, the recipe arrived in Italy. Its introductory journey continued across Europe to Britain, with its associated enjoyment was linked initially to the King Charles I era, in the 17th century. Locally, there were certainly ice cream stalls on the promenade from at least 1926, and, by the post World War Two years, there were certainly four principal ice cream sellers in the town.

Davies, Lorne Dairy The dairy operated from the Old Market Hall and a café in Market Square.

Antoniazzi's of the Penguin Café They produced Italian style ice cream, which was sold on the promenade from a three-wheeler pedal cart operated by Tom Corri. An advert of theirs declared, in 1932:

Bitchell's This ice cream was sold on the promenade from three-wheeler mobile pedal carts. Unfortunately, during 1945, an outbreak of typhoid in the town was linked with ice cream. The resulting bad publicity led to a reduced number of visitors that summer and the following year.

Ashley's Café was on 31 Marine Terrace, adjacent to the King's Hall. Its owners operated kiosks on Marine Terrace and on the beach, selling teas, soft drinks and ice cream, from the 1920s until the 1950s. Their ice cream was made on the premises.

Chalets for ice cream sales were erected at convenient spots along the promenade, two on Marine Terrace, one at Castle Point, and one opposite South Road, which survives to this day. Local ice cream manufacturers continued to sell locally up to the 1960s.

Carpinini's Mayflower Café One late interloper in the 1960s was *Sidoli's* of New Quay. The originator of one of the national ice cream distributors, Tommy Walls, lived in Borth during the early 1940s, although he isn't credited as a local producer.

NOTED FOR OUR
SPECIAL PUREST ICE CREAMS

TRY ONE OF OUR
MIXOLOGISTS ICE CREAM SODAS
IT WILL SATISFY THE THIRSTIEST PERSON

WHEN BUYING FROM AN
ICE CREAM CART SEE THAT IT IS
**ANTONIAZZI'S
PUREST GUARANTEED**

Albert Wilson, selling ice-cream to local children in Pound Place on the corner of Northgate Street, outside R P Roberts' poultry shop, is captured by the camera of Arthur Lewis. Albert Wilson lived between South Road and Trefechan Bridge. The ice cream cart would be cycled onto the promenade during the summer seasons of the 1940s.

Collection: National Library of Wales.
Photographer: Arthur Lewis 28, Great Darkgate Street, Aberystwyth

The Carpinini family with one of their three-wheeler, ice cream pedal bicycles in the 1960s. Painted on the side of them would be the well known logo, *Stop me and buy one*. Its founder, Ernest Carpinini, came initially to south Wales, soon after World War One. He later settled with his family in Portland Road, Aberystwyth, where they had their supper bar. He also opened the Mayflower Café in Terrace Road, in which he also made his Italian style ice cream. His son-in-law, Barry O'Donovan, recalls the busy summer-times spent producing the popular seasonal product.

Collection: Barry O'Donovan

The Beach Restaurant was run by the owners of Ashley's Café, next door to the King's Hall, on Marine Terrace. They also ran the Coliseum Cafeteria in Terrace Road for many years. The enterprising caterers erected this stall on the beach opposite the Royal Belle Vue Hotel during the 1920s summer seasons, offering refreshments: '*Early Morning Tea & Coffee 6 a.m., Soft drinks, Fresh fruit, Chocolate and Pure ice-cream.*'

The owners and customers pose for the camera on quite a fresh day, alongside the rowing boats that have been hauled up to the top of the beach, away from the shoreline. The Pier can be seen in the background.

Collection: David Jenkins. Photographer unknown.

ASHLEY'S OF ABERYSTWYTH

'Phone 118 *'Phone* 118

The Premier Cafe, Restaurant and Hotel.   Open from 6 a.m. till 11 p.m.

Accommodation for 200 guests in our
Spacious dining and tea rooms, which
Have unequalled and unique views of
Lovely Cardigan Bay.   Opposite Bandstand.
Everything spotlessly clean and up-to-date,
You will never regret a visit to ASHLEY'S.
SERVICE AND CIVILITY IS OUR SLOGAN.

Well Furnished Single and Double Bedrooms.   Bed and Breakfast from **6/-**

NOTE THE ADDRESS

MARINE TERRACE (Opposite Bandstand)

Ashley's of Aberystwyth, 1932

From 'Aberystwyth - The Biarritz of Wales', 1932 Official Guide and Souvenir.
Published by Aberystwyth Corporation.

Aber Prom

For over thirty years, from 1945, there was a distinct lack of eating places on the promenade, particularly in the evenings. Apart from fish and chip shops in the town, there was very little to offer visitors to the seafront throughout the year. It was possible to dine and drink alcohol in the larger hotels during the Sunday prohibition era, but only as a resident. For those hungry souls not 'in residence', the first post-war 'fast food' outlet to be open in the evenings appeared during the late 1960s. It stood on the promenade and was a Hot Dog van, run by Martin Howse of Marlek Co Ltd, who was given permission to trade on the seafront in March 1969.

Collection & Photography: Peter Henley

CARNIVAL

For many years, the town carnival was held during the first week of August, coinciding with events in the town that included a carnival ball and swimming gala. The August Bank Holiday, which used to be on the first Monday of the month, coincided with the Birmingham Fortnight, when the Midlands factories shut down and many factory workers came to Aberystwyth for a fortnight's holiday. It was also known locally as Lifeboat Day, when the decorated lifeboat, after a day on display on the promenade, would be launched, following the firing of two rockets to announce the occurrence. In front of a large crowd, Albert Davies, the Great Darkgate Street fishmonger, would dive off the end of the pier and into the sea, with great ceremony. A pleasure boat would be moored near the slipway, and the local cadets would give demonstrations of Climbing the Greasy Pole, followed by feather pillow fights on a rigged up bowsprit.

The carnival procession through the town would include tableaux on twenty or more lorries requisitioned from many sources, including Hancock's Brewery, Banton's Fruiterers, and the Great Western Railway, all hastily cleaned the night before. Many of the local businesses would enter, such as the staff of Woolworth's, Mill Street Laundry and local organisations. The town band would lead the procession through the town, followed by many costumed walkers, busily collecting money from the hosts of onlookers lining the streets. The highlight of the week would be the crowning of the Carnival Queen, who rode on her own highly decorated vehicle with her party of costumed attendants. The Mayor and Mayoress would present prizes to the winning participants at the end of the week, at the promenade bandstand.

Some years, visiting warships would anchor in the bay, offering an illuminated display in the evenings, and organised trips aboard during daylight. The week of festivities would have ended with a gala dance in the King's Hall.

Aber Prom

Following along the lines of the successful BBC Television series, *It's a Knockout*, an event was held in the 1980s on the promenade, and local contestants were invited to participate in a pre-arranged arena on the promenade, near the King's Hall.

Collection: Ceredigion Museum. Photographer unknown.

Carnival

A pyjama-clad carnival entry by the Aberystwyth Silver Band in 1990.

Photographer: Elizabeth Lloyd Jones, Bow Street.

Aber Prom

MANNEQUIN PARADE AND BEAUTY COMPETITIONS

In the 1960s, the *Daily Mirror* newspaper invited female contestants to enter their national 'Ginger Snaps' beauty competition, in which regional finalists would be chosen. The six selected contestants line up for the camera on the steps of the King's Hall entrance on Marine Terrace.

Collection: Ceredigion Museum. Photographer unknown.

During the 1960s, the promenade and bandstand became popular venues for mannequin parades and beauty competitions. In the photograph, Rose Seaton and Ann Tongue lead local fashion models out onto the walkway, followed by their colleagues wearing the latest fashions and designs.

Photographer: Pickford. Collection: Mrs Vera Jones

EARLY TRANSPORT

Horse-drawn transport that had established itself over a long period in time found itself in competition when the earliest motor-powered road vehicles arrived in the town. The first motorised taxi plied for hire in 1901 and, within ten years, an established bus and charabanc service operated between local towns, run by enterprising companies that included the Great Western Railway. By 1909, the national motoring magazine, *Auto Car* warned their readers against contemplating a trip to Aberystwyth because of its police traps, regardless of the fact that the top speed allowed then was 20 miles per hour. The Great Western Railway Company invested in new, open-topped charabancs in 1907, and operated them for summertime *Observation Car Trips* along the promenade and the coast. For the more adventurous, the Great Western Railway Company offered a six-wheeled charabanc service to the top of Plynlimon.

TOAST RACK

The Crosville Motor Company produced a specially designed, open-air, single-decker bus, with eight rows of wooden seats that ran from one side to the other. The buses had a narrow running-board, to enable people to clamber on board through the open sides, giving the vehicles the appearance of over-sized toast racks. Since there was no central gang-way, it must have been quite an effort for the conductor to collect fares. The Crosville Company modified three vehicles from a pre World War Two design and stationed them at Barmouth and Aberystwyth in 1955. They were ideal for short, low speed journeys such as promenade work. The Aberystwyth-based pair offered a circular tour of the town and promenade, starting from Park Avenue, during the summer months. Their success was short lived; they were withdrawn in 1960 and sold for scrap to a Warrington dealer.

(Details from John Pugh, Barmouth, *History of the Crosville Bus Company*)

Aber Prom

As the pleasure boats *Lizzie* and *Victory* ply for trade off Marine Terrace beach, alongside the bathing machines, an early wooden-wheeled motor car chugs its way towards a large crowd watching a morning minstrel show on the terrace, opposite the old lifeboat slipway, in the early 1900s.

Collection: Ceredigion Museum. Photographer unknown

Early Transport

An imaginary scene of a toast rack on Aberystwyth promenade in 1955.

Peter Henley

Aber Prom

One of the Crosville Motor Company's toast racks, number CFM 341, decorated as a 'Pop Shop' and full of revellers, was taking part in the Penparcau carnival in the late 1950s.

Photography: Ron Colley

A habit that has developed amongst visiting motorcyclists over the past twenty years is parking on the promenade pavement on Marine Terrace. Often, upwards of thirty motorcycles can be found parked there during summer weekends. The riders seen in the photograph, taken in August 2004, had ridden from Llanelli that day.

Collection & Photography: Peter Henley

Early Transport

For many years, from the early 1960s, the annual Round Britain Cycle Race, sponsored by the milk industry, often included Aberystwyth as one of the staging posts. The event drew over a hundred riders from Europe and was a great attraction. A section of the promenade would be cordoned off, prior to the arrival of the riders, allowing them to finish the competition stage at speed, following their 142-kilometre ride from Swansea, which took 4 hours 13 minutes. Aberystwyth became the seventh stage venue in June 1961, and the local hotels hosted the riders, support crews and the media in an overnight stop. The yellow jersey lap winner that year was Peter Chisman, with William Holmes second. The following morning, the riders were flagged away by the Mayor, Cllr. Kitchen, at the start of their day's journey to Buxton, in Derbyshire. William Holmes went on to be the overall winner of the race, with Peter coming fourth.

Collection & Photography: Peter Henley

Aber Prom

CROWDS

It was not uncommon for very large crowds to arrive in Aberystwyth annually for special events, once the town was connected to the railway system in 1864. Vast numbers, from many major towns, would pour out of excursion trains arriving at the new station. It created a problem on the promenade in 1897, forcing the Public Works Committee to erect notices on the terrace, to instruct promenaders to keep to the right. In October 1899, the *Cambrian News* reported that: *'The streets were uncomfortably crowded and hundreds of visitors could not get seats, and it is getting worse every year.'*

Some people had to be taken to Borth, to alleviate the situation. One thousand Sunday School pupils from Llanidloes were amongst the several large groups that came by train to Aberystwyth in 1902. On May Bank Holiday 1915, three thousand visitors arrived by train and, on the same day in 1919, six thousand arrived at the resort.

A comic card by the artist Lance Thakeray, posted in 1907, shows a group of males in typical Edwardian dress, lounging on seaside promenade railings and admiring a smartly dressed passing female, with the caption saying: *'They do look well after you here.'*

Collection: Peter Henley

Crowds

The vast crowds lining the promenade on August Bank Holiday 1926 fill the beach and pleasure boats. It was also Lifeboat Day, which would have included a demonstration launch of the RNLB *John and Naomi Beattie*, which was the first self-righting lifeboat to be based at the resort.

Collection: Ceredigion Museum 1986.247.1. Photographer: Frank Culliford

171

CONSTITUTION HILL

During the visit to Aberystwyth in 1896 of the Princess of Wales, her Royal Highness was invited to open and name Alexandra Hall, the University's new female student accommodation at the most northerly point of the promenade. During her visit, the Princess was invited to open the recently built Cliff Railway on Constitution Hill. Constitution Hill had become a popular venue in the late Victorian and Edwardian period, inviting to those who were capable of climbing its 400-foot elevation. For the less energetic, a ride to the top on the new funicular railway was a wonderful opportunity to enjoy the splendidly emerging view as the train climbed the steep hill. The top boasted a circular *Lunar Park*, lit with Japanese lanterns strung along the cliff-top walk. Refreshments were provided in Gothic-style, pointed-roofed pavilions, while entertainers performed in the original cliff top café. During the period of modernisation, in the late Victorian era, a switchback railway was built on the top of Constitution Hill.

The original Aberystwyth cliff railway, seen during its first decade of operation, was operated by gravity originally. An adjustment to the level of water held in large tanks attached to the front of each carriage determined the direction of movement. Both of the two carriages were connected to a single cable via a large pulley in the station at the top of the hill. As one carriage ascended, the other descended. The train is seen passing below one of the original wooden bridges on Constitution Hill, c.1900, with the brakeman standing at the controls of the descending carriage.

Photographer: Emile Thomas Evans.
Collection: Peter Henley

In about 1896, this twisting switchback railway was constructed on Constitution Hill as part of the summer attractions for those that may have ridden to the top of the hill on the new cliff railway. Its simple construction may not have offered the same level of exhilaration as some of today's fairground rides but, nevertheless, the construction certainly lasted for about ten years. Alongside it is a Victorian gazebo shelter. Date August, 1906.

Collection: Peter Davis.

Aber Prom

RELIGIOUS EVENTS

The Salvation Army was founded in 1865 and held its first meetings in Aberystwyth in 1882. Following some initial difficulty in finding a permanent meeting-place, they held open air services on the promenade. During the last decade of the 19th century, they had their own local band to accompany hymn-singing.

For many years, it was common for summer Christian services to be held on the beach. Up until the 1950s, Christian Fellowships would place a large banner on the beach and invite people to join them in makeshift, outdoor Sunday schools.

YWCA group on Aberystwyth beach

Many Welsh towns had established independent Associations protecting and promoting Christianity amongst young people. Aberystwyth had its own YWCA, the Young Women's Christian Association, in North Parade, which survived from the Victorian period into the 1990s. The YMCA, the Young Men's Christian Association, building was in Chalybeate Street and survived in use until the 1960s.

In the photograph, taken about 1900, we see a group of 120 Christian excursionists gathered on the beach and promenade, under the YWCA banner. They were probably visiting the seaside for the day and have posed for the camera a short distance from today's County Offices.

Collection: NLW. Photographer: Arthur Lewis

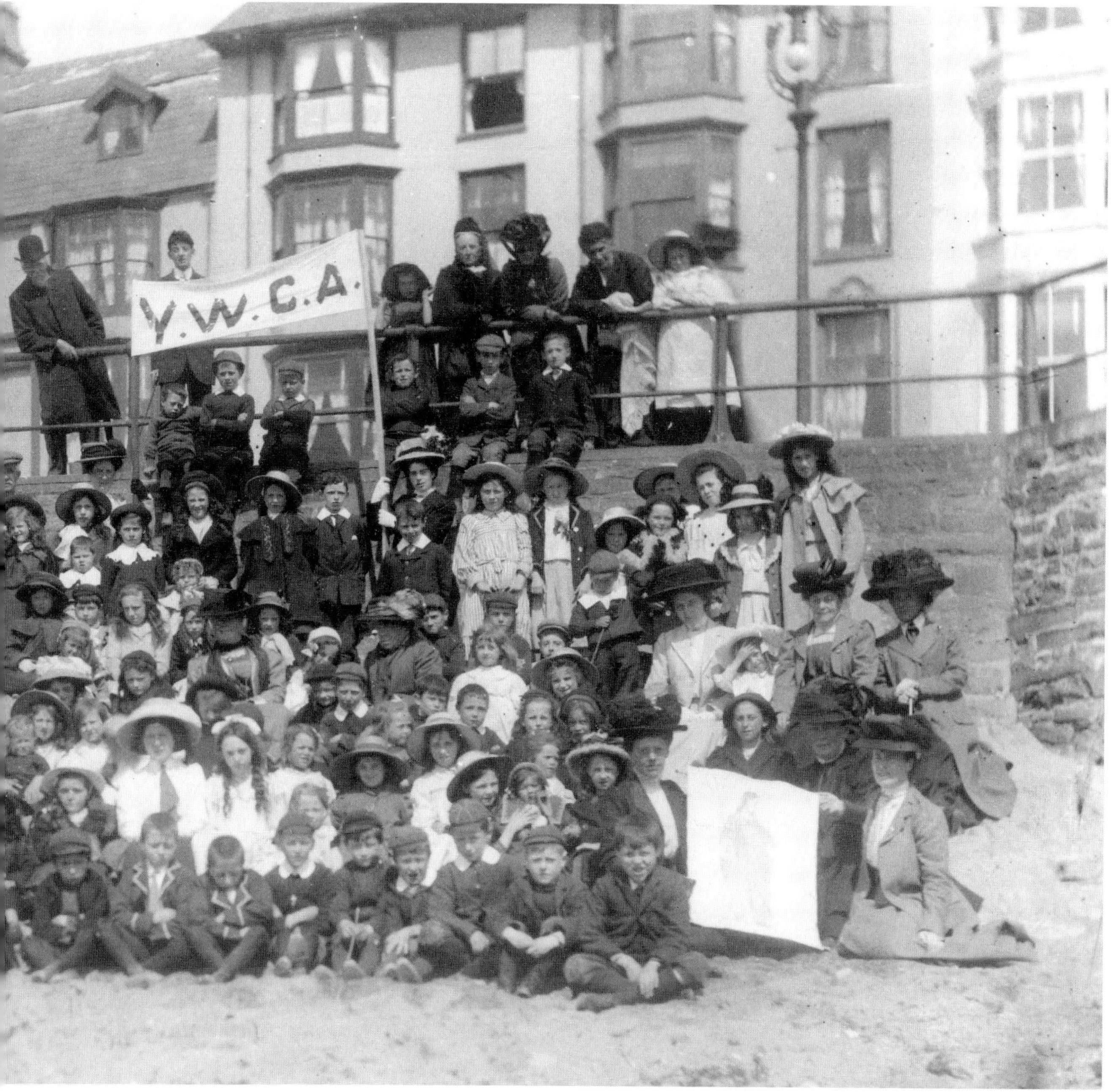
Y.W.C.A.

Aber Prom

Salvation Army poster 1882

Major Coombs of the Salvation Army in Cardiff announced on behalf of General William Booth, the national leader, that a *'Blood and Fire Bombardment of Aberystwyth,'* will take place on August 27th 1882. *'Troops will land and the war cry will be heard in the streets; Soldiers will march through the town with drawn sword; shot and shell will fall thick and fast in the enemy lines. The army Doctor will be there to attend to the wounded. Come in thousands to watch the battles,'* it invited. Insignificantly, in small print at the bottom of the poster advertising the event, it states that war with the devil will take place on the beach at 5.30 every evening that week, assisted by the *'Hallelujah Lasses'*.

Collection: Aberystwyth Town Library

Religious Events

CÔR Y CASTELL

Côr y Castell (The Castle Choir) was not a singing group with any set membership, but an informal Christian gathering characteristic of the Welsh people, who would meet together and sing for the enjoyment of Christian celebration in song. The choir originated in 1903, when the conductor of a small group, singing for their own pleasure, was approached by visitors, who suggested that he might take a collection and hand it over to a local charity. To this request the conductor acceded and the money was handed over to the Infirmary. After this, Côr y Castell steadily increased in popularity and met in the large, north-facing shelter under the castle grounds and on the opposite promenade area. The singing, every Sunday evening during the summer, and on occasional week nights, was one of the features of Welsh life that was much enjoyed by visitors from other parts of the country. Over a period of about 75 years, the organisers had collected many thousands of pounds towards local charities. The choir relocated to the bandstand in the 1970s and ceased altogether in the 1980s.

The front cover of the *Côr y Castell Collection of Welsh Hymns* for use on Sunday evenings and festivals, in 1962, price sixpence. In the front of the photograph can be seen Tom Evans (Twm Coch) selling programmes.

Collection: Peter Henley

THE UNIVERSITY AND THE PROM

On October 16th, 1872, pioneering students began their studies in Aberystwyth, in what was to be the first University in Wales. The new University College opened its doors in King's Street to the first privileged few invited to embark upon academic study. As their numbers increased, the need for and provision of student accommodation was paramount. Large halls were built, in particular, along the promenade terraces. Many of those original promenade student halls survive, some under new ownership, to this day, including Alexandra, Carpenter, Ceredigion, Hafodunus and Plynlimon. Much time would be spent by students on the promenade, particularly when en route to lectures, and a hurried return along Marine Terrace at meal-time. Initially, they were expected to wear their academic gowns in public and in lectures and then, later, during annual examinations only, up until 1965.

From its inception, a relationship was created between the people of Aberystwyth and the University which has existed harmoniously for over 130 years and has led to many joint ventures, in particular, entertainment, over the last century. Student productions would often be supported by the local authorities, with the provision of suitable venues to present dramas and other theatrical shows on the promenade, in particular, the King's Hall. In 1909, the women students, dressed up in naval-type uniforms and caps, performed locally, with HMS *Coll Girl* on their cap bands.

In his book, *The Welsh Illusion*, the well known author and broadcaster, Patrick Hannan, described Aber student days in the 1960s and the nightly, critical and passionate half hour between the pubs closing and the curfew sounding in the Women's hall of residence at 11 p.m., when the multitude of student couples that lined the north promenade railings went their separate ways. The nightly extravaganza was described by him as, necking on the railings.

The Aberystwyth students successfully ran the 'Rag', the annual charity week, in February, for many years. They sold the official Rag magazine, named at one time the *Keezle Wacka*, a satirically filled joke magazine, all over the country. Events took place daily, including a Gym Show in the King's Hall, pram races, a tower to tower race between Main College and the Penglais Llandinam buildings, kidnapping of an important member of the academic staff for ransom, and the week of events finally culminated in a procession through the town. A succession of highly decorated lorries would proceed through the town. On them different groups would create, in a very short time, a themed and colourful tableau. One well-decorated lorry would carry the Rag Queen and her attendants. There would be a great deal of mischief, including seaweed hurling, egg tossing and flour bombing between rival floats.

The University and the Prom

A group of Aberystwyth College women students dressed as *'HMS Coll Girl*s in 1909.

Collection: Peter Henley

Aber Prom

Stupendous! Magnificent!!
Unrivalled Attraction.

Infirmary Gala Night.

U.C.W. STUDENTS Present

" Merry-Go-Round "

a revue with

Evered Davies and his Band

at the

Municipal Hall, Aberystwyth

on

November 23rd. and 24th.

Two separate houses each night at 6 and 8-30 p.m.
Prices of Admission 1 6 and 1 -

PROCEEDS IN AID OF THE INFIRMARY.

Aber students regularly arranged shows that supported local charities and, in November 1934, they presented a revue entitled *Merry-Go-Round* in the brand new Municipal Hall on Marine Terrace; because the proceeds of the night were going to the local hospital, the show was called the *Infirmary Gala Night*. Collection: Ceredigion Museum AYD 8

The University and the Prom

The University Varsity Follies team of staff and students have posed themselves amongst the debris on the pier elevations, on which was the sign, 'Pier closed for repair,' following severe storms. Their costumes in the style of the pierrots were part of the annual Rag Week charity show, probably in February 1939. They are from left to right: Charles Jones, Dewi Williams, Taff Jones, Albert Evans and Neil Boughton.

Collection: Lindy Martin and Jackie Day. Photographer unknown

Aber Prom

On the University Rag Day, in February 1964, pyjama clad students are trying to protect themselves with umbrellas from bucketfuls of muddy water hurled by rival rag procession participants, outside Hafodunus Hall, on the northern end of the promenade, at Victoria Terrace.

Collection & Photographer: Peter Henley

ROYAL VISITS

Although Queen Victoria visited North Wales on many occasions, she never came to Aberystwyth. The furthest south she travelled was to Bala, in Gwynedd. Following one enjoyable stay in Wales, she instructed her private secretary to write to her eldest son, Edward, Prince of Wales, stating: *'Would Sir Henry write fully to the Prince of Wales of the excellent and enthusiastic reception we have all met with here, and to Sir F. Knollys (The Prince's secretary), to tell him how much this naturally sensitive and warm-hearted people feel the neglect shown them by the Prince of Wales and his family and that really it is very wrong of him not to come here.'* (*Aberystwyth Observer,* 1894. NLW)

The Prince of Wales, who seemingly carried the title with very little feeling, subsequently visited Aberystwyth with Princess Alexandra on June 26th, 1896, when the Prince was appointed Chancellor of the University College at Aberystwyth, while the Princess officially opened Alexandra Hall, the female students' hostel, on Victoria Terrace. On her arrival at the hall, she entered through a guard of honour of soldiers of the Royal Breconshire Volunteers and, whilst she was inside, the student choir sang for her as she was presented with a key to mark the opening. She also performed the official opening of the pier, and switched on the lights at the recently completed Cliff Railway on Constitution Hill.

In the bay, the Royal Navy had assembled ten warships from the British Channel Fleet, which created a brilliantly lit display during darkness. (*Aberystwyth Observer,* July 1896. NLW)

Other Royal visits included that of King George V and Queen Mary, who visited the Old College in 1911, when he laid the foundation stone of the National Library of Wales. His son and successor, George VI, opened part of the National Library in 1935, and drove along the promenade. As a result, the new Municipal Hall was renamed the King's Hall.

On July 11th, 1951, the Duchess of Kent, later to become Princess Marina, came to inspect the St John Ambulance Brigade and the RNLI Lifeboat crew on the promenade.

Aber Prom

Members of St John Ambulance Brigade await inspection by HRH the Duchess of Kent, on the promenade, on July 11th, 1951. Standing in front of the Boys' Brigade was their Superintendent, Mr David Blayney.

Collection: Peter Henley. Photographer: Pickford

Royal Visits

The Duchess of Kent meeting the RNLI crew of the Aberystwyth lifeboat *Lady Harrison* on Aberystwyth promenade on July 11th, 1951. Left to right: Desmond Davies; Stan Jones; the Duchess shaking the hand of Mr Daniel Thomas (Danny 'Colenzo'), the Chief Engineer; Bayden Davies and George Williams. The Duchess was accompanied by Brigadier Evans, VC, of Lovesgrove, during the inspection. On the beach behind is the *Lady Harrison* lifeboat alongside the Jubilee bandstand. This lifeboat came on station at Aberystwyth in 1949 from the RNLI Reserve fleet and served locally until 1951; it was called into rescue service on four occasions. It was replaced that year by the *Aquila Wren*.

Collection: Ceredigion Archives. Photographer: Glyn Pickford

MILITARY BANDS

Preceding the commencement of the Great War in 1914, districts surrounding Aberystwyth were used regularly for army military exercises. Camps were set up at several sites, including Lovesgrove, Clarach and Tanybwlch, and used by Welsh and English regiments. One regiment that trained here for many years was the 4th Cheshire, which incorporated many Welshmen into its ranks. For those camping at Lovesgrove, special trains allowed the soldiers and bandsmen to disembark at Bow Street station and march via Capel Dewi to set up camp in the Rheidol valley. One expected public duty of the period was the recognition of Empire Day, on Queen Victoria's birthday, May 24th. Although Queen Victoria died on January 22nd, 1901, the annual event was maintained into the reign of George V and celebrated throughout the British Empire up until 1936, when interest in its occurrence in Britain waned. The New Zealand *Oamaru Mail* reported in 1902 on the reason for celebrating Empire Day: '*The double purpose of keeping fresh and green the memory of a most illustrious reign and rejoicing in the consolidation of our great empire.*'

For many years following the Second World War the people of the town and summer visitors would be entertained by visiting military bands. An area in front of the bandstand would be cordoned off and lined with deck-chairs for viewers as the bands played and soldiers gave displays of counter marching.

In 1953, the Welsh Guards were given the freedom of the Borough of Aberystwyth and celebrated the honour again thirty years later, in 1982, when their band and Battalion of Guards visited the town and ceremoniously marched through the streets and on the promenade. In 2003, they celebrated the 50th anniversary of the honour bestowed upon them, when a contingent of Welsh Guards marched along the promenade to the War Memorial, led by the Aberystwyth Silver band.

Military Bands

The 4th Cheshire Regiment, led by their regimental band, taking the salute on Empire Day, May 24th, 1910, on Marine Terrace.

Collection: Peter Davis. Photographer unknown.

Aber Prom

The Royal Welch Fusiliers band, led by their corps of drums, parading on Aberystwyth promenade in 1961. They were led by the Pioneer Corps and the Battalion's goat mascot.

Collection & Photography: Peter Henley

Military Bands

The battalion of the Welsh Guards on Aberystwyth promenade in May 1982.

Collection & Photography: Peter Henley

NAVAL VISITS

Royal visitors to the town would often be accompanied by a fleet of warships that would moor off Aberystwyth. During the period when the British Royal Navy depended upon a substantial naval force, it was not uncommon to have a several warships from the Home Fleet visiting the resort at any one time. Remarkably, on June 20th, 1896, during the visit of the Prince of Wales and Princess Alexandra to the town, ten warships assembled off Castle Point. They included HMS *Majestic* (The flag ship, under the command of Vice Admiral Lord Walter Kerr), *Magnificent, Empress of India, Repulse, Royal Sovereign, Hermione, Resolution, Halcyon, Bellona* and *Blake*.

Due to the shallowness of the sea around Cardigan Bay, large sea-going vessels anchored a mile off shore from Castle Point. During official visits, the naval officers and crew would be welcomed ashore and invited to civic receptions by the people of the town. The last multiple visit by visiting warships was in 1955, when three ships anchored in the bay. They included an American destroyer, a Royal Navy frigate and an Irish Navy corvette. The town became transformed by shore-leave sailors and with the regular lorry loads of troops from the army camp at Tonfanau, near Towyn, in Gwynedd.

During its visit to the town from 24th to 29th June 1939, the crew of HMS *Resolution* were entertained ashore by the townspeople. Official meals, excursions and dances were arranged throughout the week. The warship's band joined in by providing music on the bandstand for a promenade open air dance. The Royal Navy battleship *Resolution* was built by Palmers in 1915 and served in both World Wars as part of the Grand Fleet. Following its official visit to Aberystwyth, it served in the Atlantic, protecting convoys during 1939-40.

It had a displacement of 28,500 tons, a top speed of 21 knots and a complement of 920 men. It became a training ship during 1944-45, and was scrapped in Faslane, in Scotland, in 1948.

The Town Council was dismayed when it discovered, during that period, that local boatmen were charging passengers one shilling (5p) to visit the ship, one-way, instead of the recommended nine pence (3.8p) for a return journey.

Naval Visits

Four of ten visiting warships are seen at anchor off Aberystwyth's Castle Point in June 1896. In the foreground can be seen the original camera obscura and meteorological station, erected in the late Victorian period. The camera obscura became a popular attraction with Victorian visitors, enabling them to see an enlarged, colourful view of the surrounding area. It consisted of a rotating prism housed above a large glass lens, which shone a focussed picture of the scenery onto a white-painted tabletop in a darkened room. The prism was rotated to scan the coastline through 360 degrees. The adjacent weather station probably housed a thermo-hydrograph for recording temperature and humidity measurements.

Collection: Ceredigion Museum AY213. Photographer unknown

In the photograph are seen Royal Navy sailors and local boatmen on the Marine Terrace slipway at Aberystwyth during the 1920s. Of the two visiting World War I warships anchored in the bay, the right hand vessel was the HMS *Valhalla*, a flotilla leader destroyer of the Valkyrie 'V' class of five ships. It was built at the Denny Brothers Clyde-side shipyard in Dumbarton, Scotland, and launched on May 22nd, 1917. It had a crew of 115, a displacement of 1,188 tons, and a top speed of 34 knots. It was finally decommissioned, surplus to requirements, and scrapped in December 1931. The boat to the left in the foreground of the photograph is the *Mauritania,* a local pleasure boat, and the adjacent vessel is a Morecambe Bay herring boat.

Incidentally, *Volunteer*, a wooden coasting ketch weighing 65 tons, was built in Aberystwyth in 1861 and from 1908 it carried coal to the Isles of Scilly. It unfortunately foundered in the Bristol Channel on the 20th of November 1911, in its 50th year of existence. Its owners saved the figurehead, which depicted a kneeling rifleman volunteer, and presented it to the Maritime Museum close to its last registered port, on the Isle of Tresco, in the Scillies. This museum at Valhalla displays a large collection of ships' figureheads, including the one off the 19th century, wooden British warship named H.M.S. *Valhalla*. In Nordic legend, the greatest Viking warriors were invited to expect a new and better eternal life in Valhalla. Collection: National Library of Wales. Photographer: Arthur Lewis.

The sailors of HMS *Valiant* are seen on the castle grounds, watching the 1934 Historical Pageant, performed from July 11-18th. The warship made an official visit to the town and its band came ashore and performed a drum-head service in the castle grounds, which was followed by a march through the town. HMS *Valiant*, seen moored in the bay behind the old coastguard hut, was a 27,500-ton member of the Queen Elizabeth battleship class, and was built in 1916 in Glasgow. It served in the Grand Fleet in the North Sea during the remainder of World War I. Following several refits in the 1930s, it later played a prominent role in WWII, serving worldwide and sustaining serious damage in the Mediterranean and in the Far East. *Valiant* returned to the UK in 1944 and was used as a training ship, before being decommissioned in 1948.

Collection: Ceredigion Museum 1985.37.4. Photographer unknown

The battleship HMS *Resolution* at Aberystwyth in June 1939.

Photographer: Maurice James Henley. Collection: Peter Henley

Naval Visits

The American Navy's stores issue ship *Antares* visited Aberystwyth on August 22-24th, 1961, during its role as support ship for ballistic missile submarines deployed abroad. It was skippered by Captain Arthur M Savage. The ship was built at Portland, Oregon, USA, and launched on May 19th, 1944. It served in the Second World War and continued to operate as a navy cargo vessel for many years afterwards, particularly in the Mediterranean. In 1958, it earned the Armed Forces Expeditionary Medal for its support during the intervention in Lebanon. It saw service also at Holy Loch, Scotland, in 1962, and in Cuba, before being decommissioned in December 1964. It was laid up at James River, Vancouver, for 11 years before being sold for scrap in 1975.

Collection & Photography: Peter Henley

AIR DISPLAYS

On June 6-7th, 1914, within eleven years of man's first flight, the *Daily Mail* sent an aeroplane to give a flying demonstration over Aberystwyth, and as further aircraft began appearing in the skies above the town in the following years, Blaendolau and Tanybwlch fields were the only suitable places for landing and taking off. No initiative was taken locally to encourage the establishment of a permanent flying base at the town, apart from allowing visiting flying circuses to come there for a short time in the 1930s, when biplane operators offered brief flights. Visits by flying boats from the 1930s until the 1950s offered promenaders new horizons.

Air Displays

Sea plane at Aberystwyth.

RAF Supermarine Southampton II flying boat number 1643 of 201 Squadron was photographed at anchor off Aberystwyth promenade in the summer of 1934. In that year, the squadron left its base at Calshot, Stanswood Bay, in the Solent, to move north to Stranraer, Loch Ryan, in west Scotland. It is likely that the flight would have included a stop-over at Aberystwyth on a 'showing the flag' route as the aircraft headed north along the coastline.

The dockland area of Pembroke was chosen as a base for RAF Coastal Command flying boats during the Second World War. The principle choice of aircraft was the Sunderland, built by Short Brothers of Belfast, and powered by 4 powerful Pegasus engines. These large, elegant aircraft served as reconnaissance, rescue and submarine attack aircraft, covering the western Atlantic approaches and the Irish Sea. Several peacetime visits were made to Aberystwyth following the war. In the early 1950s, three Sunderland flying boats anchored in the bay, off the promenade, for several days. One example, repatriated from the French Navy, is now preserved at the RAF Museum in Hendon.

Collection: Ceredigion Museum. Photographer unknown.

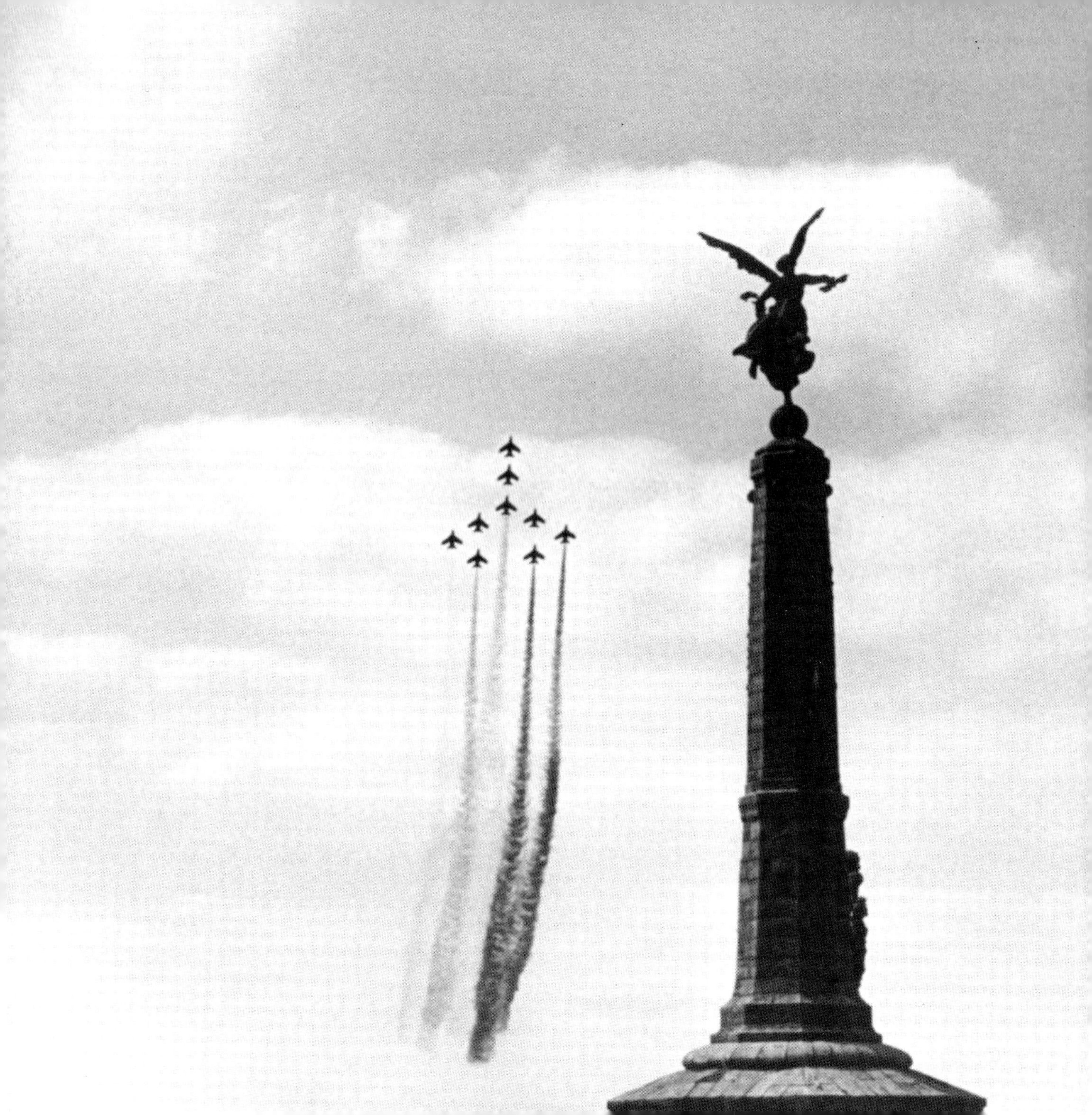

Air Displays

The Red Arrows aerobatic team climb vertically through the clouds above the sea off Castle Point. The squadron was based at RAF Fairford, in Gloucestershire, and consisted of a formation of nine red-painted Folland Gnat jet trainer aircraft. In the foreground is the 1922-built memorial commemorating the servicemen and women who were lost in the two World Wars. The memorial and statues representing peace were designed by the celebrated Italian sculptor Mario Rutelli (1859-1941) for Aberystwyth.

Photography: Peter Henley.

On July 2nd, 1969, the Royal Navy combined with the Royal National Lifeboat Institution at Aberystwyth to give a demonstration of an air-sea rescue near the pier. The helicopter taking part was Westland Whirlwind type HAS.7 number HN311-14, based at RAF Brawdy, in Pembrokeshire. The Aberystwyth lifeboat taking part was the D Class inshore rescue boat number 28, manned by Gwyn Martin and Peter Henley. The third lifeboat crew member in the sea, about to be 'rescued', is Michael Nicholls, son of the last Coxswain of the *Aquila Wren* lifeboat, John Nicholls.

Photography: Peter Henley.

HANG-GLIDING

Although UK hang-glider manufacturing began in 1971, hang-gliding in Wales was still in its infancy in 1980. One of the pioneer pilots in the principality was Rod Lees from Capel Bangor, who now lives in Australia. In the photograph, he is seen gliding over the promenade in 1981, in a Typhoon glider made in 1980 by the Solar Wings Company in Marlborough, Wiltshire. The first ever Celtic Cup hang-gliding competition was held on Constitution Hill in 1980 and has now become a major event, held annually in each of the Celtic Countries. A recent venue for the event was in Iceland. The interest in conventional hang-gliding has waned in the last few years, due to the increasing popularity of paragliding. (Information: Patrick Laverty of Talybont, the former UK hang-gliding distance record holder (Cemmaes to Grantham Lincolnshire) 1986-89. Incidentally, the photograph represents the brief period in 1981 when no beach slipway existed.)

Rod Lees, flying a Typhoon hang glider, gives a demonstration flight over Marine Terrace in 1981.

Collection and photography: Peter Henley

ABERYSTWYTH LIFEBOAT

The earliest British coastal lifeboats appeared in the late 18th century, during the early stages of the Industrial Revolution, with the establishment of a British Lifeboat Service during the years 1770-1820. An Institution was formed, albeit with little funds, and survived until 1854, when the Institution was renamed The National Shipwreck Institution. It re-emerged soon afterwards as the Royal National Lifeboat Institution. By 1895 there were 308 lifeboats in service around the country, and all made to very much the same design: a 35-foot rowing boat. A lifeboat was purchased for Aberystwyth in 1843, by public subscription, and, in 1861, an auxiliary branch of the RNLI was formed. A lifeboat was delivered from London via Bristol and became the first of a succession of five rowing and sailing lifeboats to be based at the town. The first engine-powered lifeboat was commissioned here in 1932.

In 1875, Aberystwyth had its own lifeboat house built, a conventionally constructed building to a standard RNLI design, in Queen's Road, near today's tennis courts. It exists in the 21st century very much as it was built, although redundant as a lifeboat house since 1965. It was designed by the Honorary Architect to the RNLI, Mr C H Cooke.

In 1963, the RNLI stationed one of its first inshore inflatable rescue boats (IRBs) at Aberystwyth, making a change in the station's 100-year-history. The new lifeboats, known as the 'D' class, measured 15.5 feet and became known as Rubber Ducks, although their official title was Inshore Lifeboats (ILBs). The new lifeboat became full-time locally following the withdrawal of the *Aquila Wren* in 1964. At this time, the ILBs were the fastest boats in lifeboat service and were powered by a single American Evinrude, 40-horse-powered, outboard engine capable of 20 knots. The hull was constructed of neoprene-proofed nylon with marine ply panels and had six buoyancy bags. It had the capability of being launched very quickly off a wheeled trailer, from the relatively sheltered waters of the harbour, rather than from the exposed Marine Terrace beach. It was also able to approach rocky shorelines with less risk of damage to its hull. It now suited the more frequent inshore type of emergency, common with swimmers, local boating and cliff rescue, rather than the now less common offshore shipping problems, which are handled by the larger Newquay and Barmouth lifeboats. The very first of these D Class boats in service locally was donated by the customers of the London public house, the *Rising Sun* and was stationed here as the first RNLI inflatable lifeboat in Britain. It was called into service 208 times and saved 143 lives from the clutches of Cardigan Bay.

In 1973, a later inflatable lifeboat proved its

Aberystwyth Lifeboat

ability in shallow water, when it was launched 3 miles inland, at Lovesgrove, to assist in the rescue of people from a flooded caravan site following heavy rain. In 1983, the ILB was superseded by the new C Class lifeboat, which offered a night capability search and rescue. Until 2006, the Aberystwyth lifeboat was an Atlantic 75, capable of 32 knots. Its replacement in 2007 will be one of the latest breed of inshore rescue boats.

Between 1903 and 1910, the Royal National Lifeboat Institution stationed a temporary lifeboat at Aberystwyth. It was called 'LILY BIRD, RESERVE No. 5, named after the daughter of the donor, Samuel Bird. It was built in 1894 as a 34-foot pulling and sailing, self-righter by the London firm of Forrest at a cost of £389. It served initially at Dunwich, on the Suffolk coast, south of Lowestoft, from 1894-1903. Following its relief duty at Aberystwyth, it sailed to St Helier on Jersey, in the Channel Islands, where it served from 1910 to 1912. In the photograph, taken on Aberystwyth beach, the Coxswain, David Williams, and his crew, are accompanied by the Honorary Secretary, Captain Doughton. The photograph could have been taken following the departure of the RNLB *Elisabeth Lloyd* and before the commissioning of the *John and Naomi Beattie* in 1906.

Photographer: Emile Thomas Evans. Collection: Peter Henley

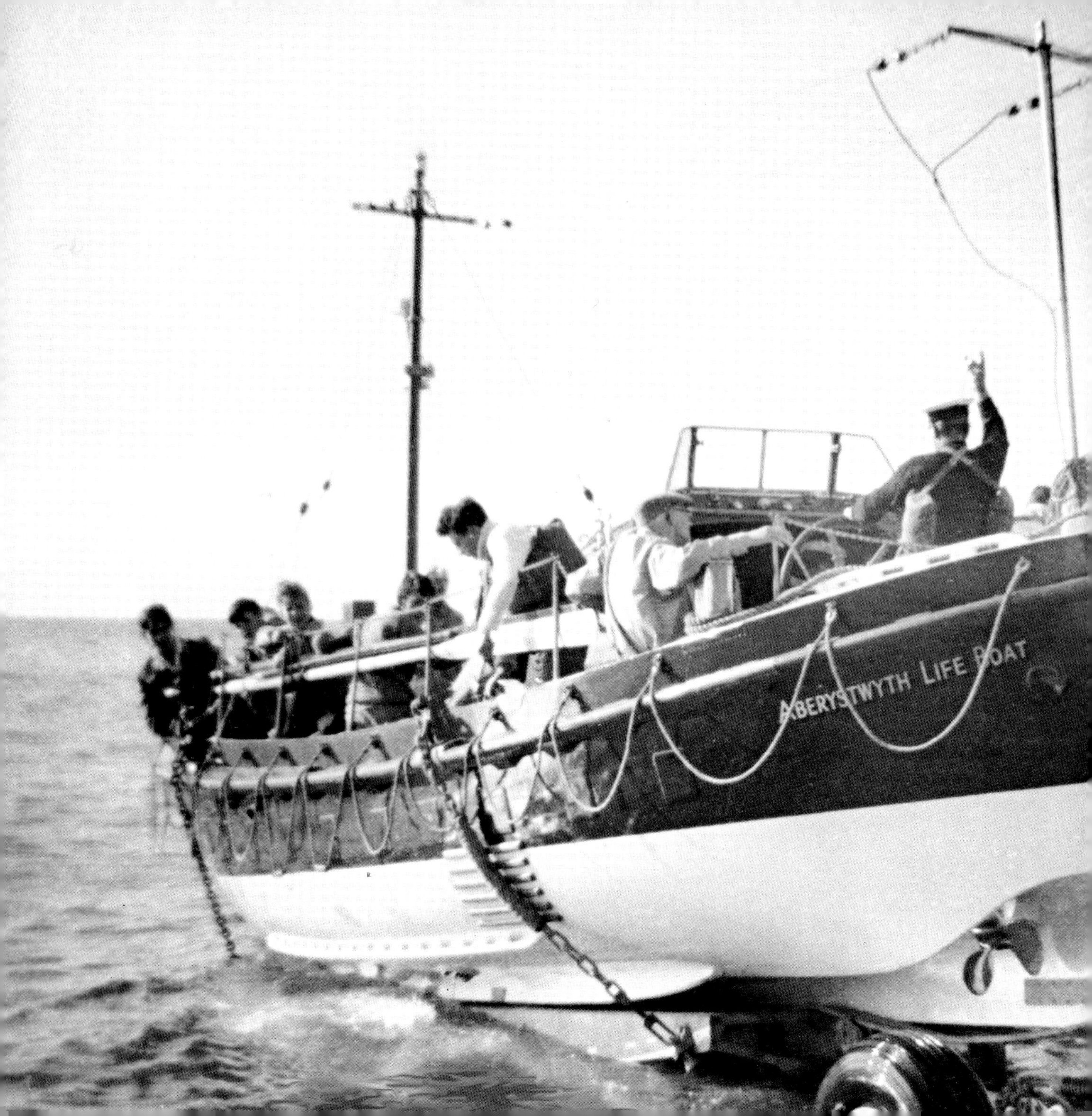
ABERYSTWYTH LIFE BOAT

Aberystwyth Lifeboat

The *Aquila Wren*, a member of the 35-foot Liverpool class, was commissioned as the Aberystwyth Lifeboat in 1951, in memory of twenty-two members of the Women's Royal Navy Service who lost their lives in the S.S. *Aquila* in 1941. The lifeboat was a gift of the Aquila Wrens Memorial Fund and a legacy of Mr J Moorehouse of St Anne's-on-Sea, Lancashire. The lifeboat served at Aberystwyth from 1951 to 1964 and, during that time, it saved 14 lives and was launched 21 times. It was the first local lifeboat not to be equipped with sails and the first to be twin screwed. In the photograph, taken on Lifeboat Day 1962, the Coxswain, Bayden Powell Davies, prepares for launching from the caterpillar trailer on Marine Terrace beach.

Collection & Photography: Peter Henley.

Two young members of the RNLI crew, David Rowe and Charlie Downes, both of Aberystwyth, are seen on board the *Aquila Wren,* prior to launching on an August Lifeboat Day, c. 1962.

Photography: Peter Henley

Following its return from duty at sea, the RNLB *Aquila Wren* is prepared on the beach in front of the King's Hall, for its return to the lifeboat station in Queen's Road, c. 1961. The Coxswain, Bayden Davies, discusses the procedure with the RNLI Honorary Secretary, Harold Evans, on the left, while Captain Brodigan checks the securing chains. John Nicholls is heading towards the stern with Evan Daniels. Several other crew members, including Ron Hutchings and Dilwyn Evans, assist in the impending movement.

Photographer: David Henley.

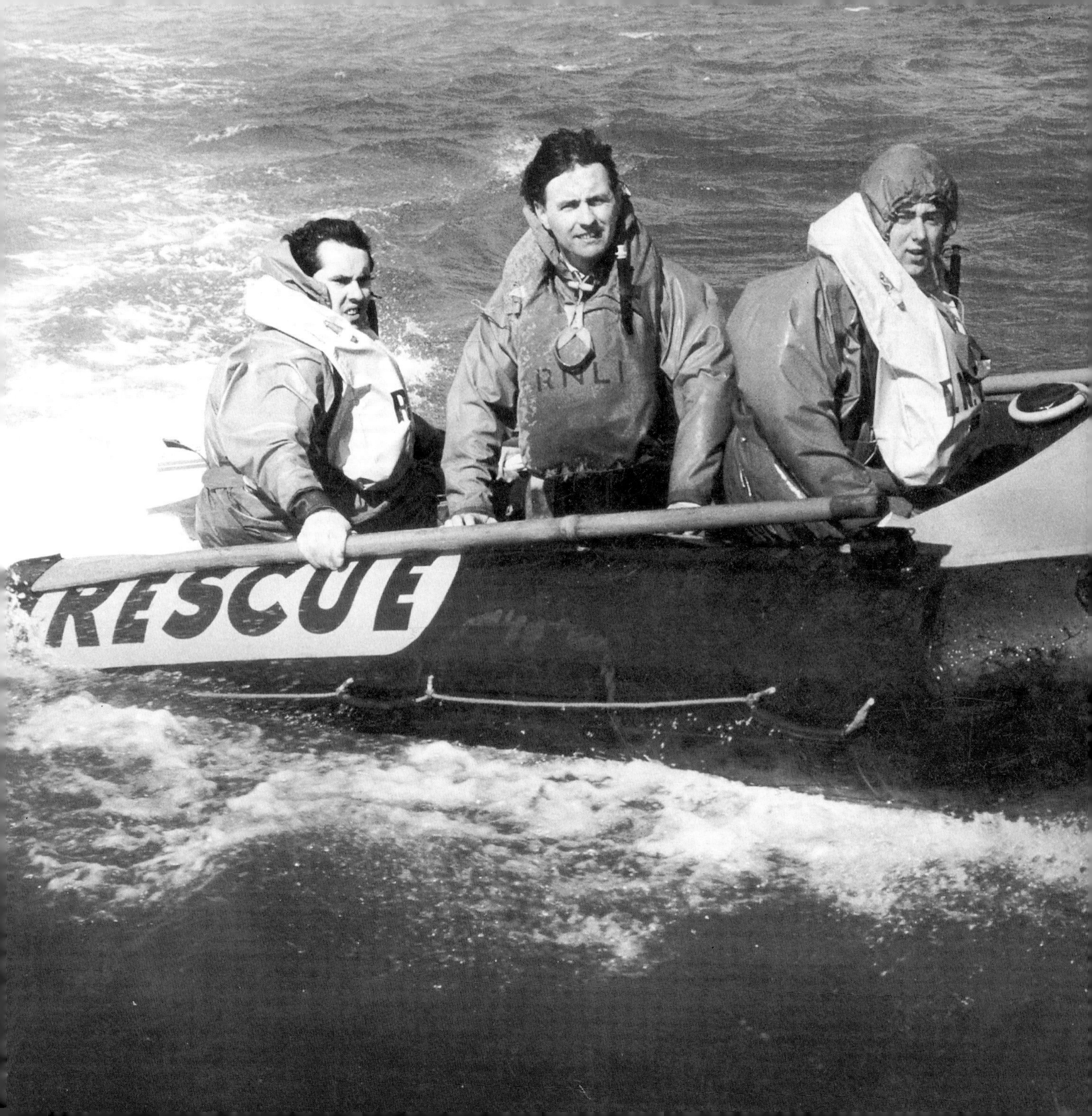
RNLI
RESCUE

The Aberystwyth lifeboat D 186 in 1965, on duty with crew members, Jeff Davies, Peter Henley and Tommy Ridgeway.

Collection: Peter Henley.
Photographer: Gwyn Martin

Aber Prom

BEACH LIFESAVING

The Aberystwyth Surf Lifesaving Club was formed in 1966 by a volunteer group keen to provide a lifesaving service on Aberystwyth beach. The teenagers trained using the reel and line method of surf lifesaving and teams of six were employed initially by the Borough Council as Life Guards. During the summer, under the guidance of one full-time guard, Paul Kidson, they helped to ensure that the beach was one of the safest in the country.

On the main beach, opposite Marine Terrace, and on the south beach, flags would be raised on poles, informing swimmers of current sea conditions. The club, on several occasions, represented Wales in National Championships in surf exercises. Younger members of the club were in two groups: cadets and juniors, with ages ranging from ten to fifteen. During the early days, a hut was erected on the promenade as a club headquarters and used to store their equipment, which had been paid for from funds collected by the boys themselves.

The rescue team of four bringing a 'casualty' ashore during a lifesaving exercise on Aberystwyth beach using the reel and line retrieval method.

Photo: Peter Henley

Beach Lifesaving

The 1967 Aberystwyth Surf Lifesaving Club members' team preparing to rehearse on Aberystwyth beach. They include, from left to right: Paul Norrington-Davies, Mel Jones, Elwyn Isaac, Richard Arthur, Paul Kitson and Peter Norrington-Davies. Also in the photograph is the official photographer, Glyn Pickford of Pier Street.

Photography: Peter Henley

KICKING THE BAR

Many questions have been asked about the origins of the local tradition of 'kicking the bar' at Aberystwyth. Why do people do it, when was it started, and by whom? Some suggest that the college students started the habit adjacent to their halls of residence, and some do it simply to bring good luck. Whatever the answer is, I believe it must remain one of those unsolved mysteries, left to those who enjoyed kicking the bar and to those who will continue to do so into the future. To add confusion, there have been two 'bars' at the northern end of the promenade, at Victoria Terrace. The original Victorian, round-turreted end was swept away during two violent storms in 1938, along with a length of promenade up to the cellars of the halls of residence and houses. The sea wall and walkway were substantially reinstated 65 years ago and survive today, with the modified, modern, square end to the promenade with a low, white-painted hand rail, which, of course, is *the bar*.

Kicking the Bar

Kicking the bar at Aberystwyth. At the northern end of Aberystwyth promenade, at Victoria Terrace, are teenagers Sian and Gwenno Henley, 'kicking the bar' in September 2003.

Photography: Peter Henley

Aber Prom

The promenade was extended northwards in the early Victorian period and ended close to Constitution Hill with a round turreted construction with seats and railings. A wooden water breaker with a walkway on it ran from the sea wall seaward. In this Edwardian scene, visitors are seen enjoying the summer weather some time in the first few years of the 20th century. The structure survived until 1938.

Photographer: Emile Thomas Evans.
Collection: Peter Henley

SEAGULLS

Awarding themselves the pleasure of privileged positions on the harbour promenade railings, towards sunset, herring gulls, nobly set apart from the nearby starlings, gather to socialise before retiring. Other seagulls are always close by, from the Laridae family, including the black-headed gull and the wide-winged, lesser black-backed gull. All of them, from the earliest days of the promenade and before, have always regarded themselves as part of its development, with an imposed natural inclusion in the continuing celebration of its existence. They will always be there, with their raucous, early morning scream, acrobatic flight and scavenging eye, effortlessly circling on the lookout for a tasty morsel.

Photography: Peter Henley

'The idea of leaving Aberystwyth simply makes me cry.' A Donald McGill comic postcard sent from Aberystwyth in 1919.

Collection: Peter Henley

'If you want value for your money come here'. 'At Aberystwyth'. Posted at Aberystwyth on July 26th, 1921.

Collection: Ann Lucas

REFERENCES

1. Entertainment in Aberystwyth 1780-1977- R F Walker. In the book *ABERYSTWYTH 1277-1977,* Gomer Press (1977).
2. *The Story of the Harp in Wales,* Osian Ellis (1991), University of Wales Press.
3. *Valley of Song – Music and Society in Wales 1840-1914,* Gareth Williams (1998), University of Wales Press, Cardiff.
4. *Aberystwyth 1277-1977,* Afan ab Alun (1977), Y Lolfa, Talybont
5. Ceredigion Volume XIII No. 1 (1997) Photo of Aber Band marching up Great Darkgate Street c. 1890 in 'Friendly societies in Aberystwyth and their contribution towards cultural and social life, Emma Lile.
6. *'Some special aspects of the physical and social structure of nineteenth century Aberystwyth* (In Aberystwyth Public Reference Library.) Harold Carter and Sandra Wheatley, (1977), UWA Department of Geography, Aberystwyth.
7. The Great War in Wales: Memory and Monuments in Ceredigion, Angela Gaffney (2001), published in 'Ceredigion' Volume XIV number 1.
8. A photograph of Aberystwyth pier from 'An Illustrated History of Cardiganshire', W J Lewis (1970).
9. Extracts from *'The Entertainers'* Frances Wilkins (1973), Allman and Son Ltd, London.
10. Extracts from *'Villages and Town Bands'* Christopher Wier (1981), Shire Publications Ltd.
11. Extract from *'Oh, Listen to the Band'* Kenneth Cook (1950), Hinrichsen Edition Ltd.
12. Extracts from *'Labour and Love, an oral history of the Brass Band movement* Arthur R. Taylor, Elm Tree Books Limited, London.
13. Photographs from *'Aberystwyth Yesterday'* Howard C Jones (1980), Stewart William Publishers, Barry, South Glamorgan.
14. Extracts from 'A Town Band by Design' An exploration of Aberystwyth Town Band's Formative years 1890-1894' Felicity Fitchard, B.A. Honours Dissertation 1994, History Department, University of Wales, Aberystwyth.
15. Extracts from '*Y Delyn yng Nghymru, The Harp in Wales*' D Roy Saer, (1991) Welsh Folk Museum, Gomer Press in association with the National Museum of Wales.
16. '*Aberystwyth 1277-1977, eight lectures to celebrate the seventh centenary of the foundation of the borough*. Edited by Ieuan Gwynedd Jones (1977), Gomer Press.
17. Extracts from '*Aberystwyth' A portrait in old picture postcards*, William Troughton (1989), S.B Publications
18. Extract from *Aberystwyth Borough 1277 – 1974* Howard C Jones (1974), *The Cambrian.*
19. Extracts from '*Beside the Seaside*' James Walvin (1978), Allen lane Printers.
20. Details from 'Model of Aberystwyth about 1340' produced by Ceredigion District Council Ceredigion Museum.
21. Extracts from '*A History of Wales*' Volume One, J E Lloyd (1911), Longmans.
22. Quotations from 'Golden memories of days gone by' by Howard C. Jones, *Western Mail* April 12th 1980.
23. Extracts from 'The Maritime heritage of some southern Ceredigion villages' by J. Geraint Jenkins, Welsh Industrial and Maritime museum, Cardiff. Published in 'Ceredigion' Journal of the Ceredigion Antiquarian Society Volume 1X Number 2 (1981).
24. Extracts from '*The Welsh Illusion*' Patrick Hannan (1999), Poetry Wales Press Limited, Bridgend.
25. References from '*The Welsh King and his Court*' published on behalf of the History and Law Committee of the Board of Celtic Studies, University of Wales Press (2000).
26. *Anatomy of Wales,* Owain T. Edwards, Chapter X1 Page 223.
27. Conversation with Danny Parry.
28. Conversation with George Lewis, 39 Portland Road, about pleasure boats and loan of photographs.
29. Conversation with Mrs Phillips, 28 Portland Road, about Jack Price.
30. Conversation with Reg White and Philip Lewis in Reg's house, Greenfield Street.
31. Rhidian Griffiths, NLW, for programmes of Aber concerts etc. and for reading the Music introduction in chapter 4.
32. David E Jenkins, conversation about lifeboats and help with local maritime history.

References

33. Hywel T Jones, conversation about the Aberystwyth town bands.
34. Extracts from an article entitled 'Aberystwyth Lifeboats' by Joan Davies, published in the journal of the Royal National Lifeboat Institution, 'The Lifeboat' Winter 1984/85 Volume XLIX Number 490.
35. Extracts from Navyhistory.com about USS *Antares*.
36. Extracts from www.dewielersite.net about the 1961 Milk Race.
37. Historical Manuscripts Commission - details of Aberystwyth & Aberdovey Steam Packet Co. Ltd.
38. Details from www.naval-art.com about HMS *Valiant*.
39. Details from 'Lifeboats' by Nicholas Leach. A Shire Album number 336.
40. Details from 'Lifeboats' by Nicholas Leach, (1998) a Shire Album.
41. Loan of photographs and conversation with Evan Andrews, South Road, Aberystwyth.
42. Loan of photographs and conversation with Mrs Lillian Bates of Rheidol View, Aberystwyth.
43. Dr Joanna Archibald, Heritage Manager of the RNLI Headquarters, Poole, for lifeboat history details.
44. Mr Barry Fox, Honorary Librarian RNLI, for lifeboat historical details.
45. Mr Richard Emlyn Edwards, for the use of historical memoirs of the Sea Cadet Corps and Uncle Tommy.
46. Peter and Paul Norrington Davies and Mr Jeff James, for information regarding the Surf Lifesaving Club.
47. Mr Frank Collison, for information about Captain John Rees, master of the *Birmingham City* pleasure boat.
48. Mrs Vera Jones, Plas y Brenin, Aberystwyth. Loan of photographs and conversations.
49. Mr Tom Parry Edwards and Mrs Meinir Holliday, Abermagwr, for historical information.
50. Mr Will Owen, BBC Wales Cardiff, for information on '*Y Pelydrau*'.
51. Miss Elin Wyn Davies, BBC Cymru'r Byd, for help with musical group history.
52. Loan of prom harpist photograph by Mrs Shirley Davies, Prospect Street.
53. Marita Pugh for information about Peggy Royston Dancers.
54. Mrs Olga Edwards for information about the Xenons.
55. William Troughton, NLW, for many photographic researches and information.
56. Miss Chris Street for help sourcing sea cadet information.
57. David Simkin, Brighton, on history of beach photographers.
58. Patrick Laverty, Talybont, and Nick Walker, providing history of local hang gliding and providing aerial photographs.
59. Colonel Peter Crocker, Caernarfon Regimental Museum, for information about the RWF Bands.
60. Peter Davis, Aberarth, for the loan of several postcards.
61. References from 'Pom Poms and Ruffles' G F Mellor (1964), Dalesman.
62. The Festival of Britain Society secretary, Mr George Simmer, for help about the 'Guinness clock'.
63. Mr Richard Simpson, Keeper of Aircraft and Exhibits at RAF Museum Hendon, for identifying flying boats.
64. Extracts from '*Seaside Architecture*' Kenneth Lindley, Hugh Evelyn Ltd. Page 58 'The Mutoscope'.
65. Mr Brain Lile, for local band references in NLW etc., and in his book, '*The Old Black and Green' Aber Town F.C. 1884-1984*, written with Peter Parry.
66. Extracts from Dancer History Archives by Streetswing.com on T.D. Rice.
67. Extracts from 'The Waits', www.leziate.demon.co.uk, webmaster Chris Gutteridge.
68. Extracts from 'The Worldwide friends of Punch and Judy', web site by Glyn Edwards.
69. Stella 'software for teaching English language and literature and its assessment' web site on Pierrot Seaside entertainers.
70. Extracts from *The illustrated Victorian song book* web site by John Abbott on 'Gilbert Rogers'.
71. Extracts from 'Lit'n deb and other Victorian survivals' 1921-25 by May Cotton (nee Newing), Reminiscences of student life in Aberystwyth.
72. Extracts from 'Looking back' by D.J. Llewelfryn Davies on his student days in Aberystwyth.
73. Extracts from 'A 116th garland of British light music composers' by Philip L. Scowcroft www.musicweb.uk.net on Jimmy Leach.

Aber Prom

74. Conversation with Ron Colley Aberystwyth on local events.
75. Extracts from *Military bands and their uniforms* Jack Casson-Scott & John Fabb (1978), Blandford Press.
76. Extracts from *The Brass Band*, Harold C Hind (1934), Hawkes & Son, London
77. Extracts from *Kneller Hall; A 100 years of Military Music*, Lt Colonel P L Binns (1959), Blackmore Press, Gillingham, Dorset.
78. Mr John Pritchard Evans, Penglais, Aberystwyth, for first hand information and the loan of several books on military bands.
79. Extracts from 'Minstrels' web site www.geocities.com on minstrels and troubadours.
80. Lindy Martin, for use of photograph 'Pierrots on pier' (c. 1924) from the late Gwyn and Marjorie Martin collection.
81. Extracts from *Pavilions on the Sea* Cyril Bainbridge (1986), Robert Hale, London.
82. Details of RAF aircraft from Richard Simpson, Keeper of Aircraft and Exhibits at the RAF Museum at Hendon.
83. Details from the Aberystwyth RNLI Commemorative brochure 1983/84.
84. Aberystwyth 1931 guide book from M J Mytton.
85. Mr Max Tyler, Historian of The British Music Hall Society, loan of entertainer postcards.
86. Extracts about beach chairs from the 'Designboom' web site on 'The history of the folding chair'.
87. Mrs Fay Brown of Ventnor, IOW, for details of Victor Fleming.
88. Details from the book '*Cyfartha and the Crawshays*' Iris Roderick Thomas (1999), New Horizon Publications.

SUNSET
Do not go gentle into that good night,
Old age should burn and rave at close of day;
Rage, rage against the dying of the light.

An extract from a poem by Dylan Thomas (1914-53)

A late afternoon winter sun setting over Cardigan Bay silhouettes Rutelli's majestic angel in its silent vigil of peace. This magnificent memorial to those from the town who gave their lives for their country, stands as a guardian overlooking the sea on Aberystwyth Castle Point. February 19th, 2004.

Photographer: Sarah Jayne Henley

Also available from Y Lolfa

Cip yn ôl ar yr Hen Ffordd Gymreig o Fyw
Cefn Gwlad Geoff Charles
IOAN ROBERTS

£12.95

O Ben yr Aber
O. T. Evans (Owain Ceri)

£4.95

Aberdyfi: Past & Present

dinas

by Hugh M. Lewis M.B.E.

£6.95

For a full list of publications, ask for your free copy of our new Catalogue – or simply surf into our secure website, **www.ylolfa.com**, where you may order on-line.

y Lolfa

Talybont, Ceredigion, Cymru (Wales) SY24 5AP
ebost ylolfa@ylolfa.com
gwefan www.ylolfa.com
ffôn (01970) 832304
ffacs 832782